A Tartan Scottie Book

A Tartan Scottie Book published by Tartan Scottie Press

Copyright © 2000 by Joseph Harvill

All rights reserved under International and Pan-American Copyright Conventions. No part of this book may be reproduced in any form or by any means without permission in writing from the publisher, except for brief quotations in printed reviews. For information, or to order books, contact Tartan Scottie Press, 1028 Girard Blvd., NE, Albuquerque, NM 87106-2048. Website: www.tartanscottie.com. Phone: 505/ 266-7211. E-mail: scottie@tartanscottie.com.

Library of Congress Cataloging-in-Publication Data
Harvill, Joseph, 1944-
    The Good Life Begins with a Scottie / Joseph Harvill, editor.
    p. cm
    Summary: Bonding with Scottish Terriers requires understanding, nurturing, and celebration. Investing one's mind, heart, and will leads to quality companionship and the Scottie good life.

    Includes bibliographical references and index.
    ISBN 0-9703701-0-5
    1. Pets.   2. Dogs—Psychology.   3. Dogs—Scottish Terrier
    4. Human Ecology.   5. Companionship—Canine/Human
    I. Title.

Manufactured in the United States of America

First printing, October 2000

ISBN   0-9703701-0-5

10 9 8 7 6 5 4 3 2

Joseph Harvill, Ph.D., Editor

The Good Life Begins with a Scottie

Tartan Scottie Press
Albuquerque, New Mexico

Dedication

To 'Miss Nati' who first taught me to celebrate the Scottie good life and who now waits for 'the Girard Gang' at the Bridge, to 'Gus' and 'Willie' who are longsuffering in my awkward human attempts to grow into their great-souled character, to all the subscribers to **Great Scots Magazine** who know how to celebrate their dogs, and to Charlotte who quietly holds it all together.

TABLE OF CONTENTS

Acknowledgments   page vii
Preface   page viii

Part One: Understanding the Scottie Good Life

Chapter One
The Land and Its Dog   page 12

Chapter Two
The Scottie M.Y.S.T.I.Q.U.E.   page 18

Chapter Three
Good Dogs Are Made Not Born   page 25

Chapter Four
The Scottie Crazies and the Ties That Bind   page 32

Chapter Five
Scottie Wisdom For the New Millennium   page 38

Part Two: Nurturing the Scottie Good Life

Chapter Six
Test Your Scottie Quotient   page 47

Chapter Seven
Well-Begun Is Half-Done: Finding the Right Scottie Puppy   page 56

Chapter Eight
Puppy Bootcamp   page 61

Chapter Nine
On Loving A 'Demon' Puppy   page 72

Chapter Ten
... And Baby Makes Four: A Case Study   page 77

Chapter Eleven
Shortcourse In Walking the Dog   page 83

Chapter Twelve
11 Rules For Growing Old Scottily   page 88

Chapter Thirteen
Each Day A Victory:
Living With Scottie Cancer   page 94

Chapter Fourteen
The Art of Loving Well   page 100
Chapter Fifteen
Rewards: Inside the Pay-offs of
Scottie Love   page 104

Part Three: Celebrating the Scottie Good Life
(a) Recounting the Sunshine

Chapter Sixteen
McKnight and a Damsel in Distress   page 114
Chapter Seventeen
Bird Dog with a Brogue   page 121
Chapter Eighteen
Only A Bump In the Road: Jet,
The Paraplegic Scottie   page 127
Chapter Nineteen
June Bug Therapy   page 131
Chapter Twenty
Zoe: God's Administrative Assistant   page 136
Chapter Twenty-One
Shorty. The Infantry Mascot Who
Fought in WWII   page 140

(b) Redeeming the Shadows

Chapter Twenty-Two
Why Do I Hurt So Much? A Look Inside the Pain
of Scottie Loss   page 150
Chapter Twenty-Three
A Love Letter   page 157
Chapter Twenty-Four
Loving Angus: A Journey of the Heart   page 160
Chapter Twenty-Five
Requiem For A Dog Named Sam   page 165

Afterword
A Parable For Our Times   page 176

Appendix: Breed Bibliography   p 182

Index   page 184

Acknowledgments

An eloquent, silver-haired speaker once was asked how long his speech took to prepare. "About sixty-nine years," was his answer.

Books are like that, too, since their prologue is the whole of one's life. To one and all, both canine and human, whose sunshine or shadow colored my sense of what counts, I am grateful.

My parents are present in the pages of this book. Their influence pointed me early toward the celebration of dogs. They were not dog people in the technical sense but they were great 'fanciers' of companionship. In my early days when I was forever bringing home 'strays' found in my ramblings they always recognized and nurtured authentic dog love in a boy's wide eyes. "He's doggin' again," my mother would say. My guess is they are whispering that phrase to each other right now at the Rainbow Bridge.

Others helped with this project, too. My thanks and praise to those seven authors whose published work in *Great Scots Magazine* is included along with my own in this *GSM* anthology. Theirs is the best sort of dog writing: drawn from intimate experience of Scotties and from the wells of their hearts. My special thanks to Carole Fry Owen, of Temple, Texas, and to Margot Rosenberg and Bern Marcowitz of **Dog Lovers Bookshop**, New York City, and to Miss Betty Penn-Bull, Slough, England, who read the draft manuscript and gave me knowledgeable and encouraging feedback. Thanks also to my mother-in-law, Ann Johnson, who helped with proof-reading early drafts of the manuscript.

Most of all my thanks to my wife, Charlotte, who wanted this project before I did and whose unstinting support in all things connected with *GSM* is the enthusiastic encouragement of one who loves, and is loved by, great dogs!

Preface

There are many definitions of the good life. This book records expressions of one of them.

Buddha taught that kindness to all living things is the true religion. Philosopher Franz Kafka narrowed the Buddha's scope when he argued "All knowledge, the totality of all questions and answers, is contained in the dog."

The Greek philosopher, Diogenes, would have agreed. He loved dogs and referred to himself as "hound of heaven" and taught that the simple life is the virtuous life. To him 'going to the dogs' was a good thing.

The message of this book is simpler, still. Here ordinary voices express the conclusion of those who have found the good life in the company of one special breed of dog— the Scottish Terrier. Our conviction is summed up in the claim: "To love a dog is good. To love a terrier is better. To love a Scottie is best!"

To the writers in this book Scotties belong at the core of our good life. It is our experience that the good life is not a destination but a journey of the heart and has more to do with passions and commitments, with shared soul-making and visions of the spirit, than with money or places or things. Put simply, to us the good life is the life which has the timeless within it. We have discovered it is there, in the realm of the timeless, that we learn the deep things about our Scotties and ourselves. Because the Scottie-shaped holes our dogs leave at our center are timeless memorials to profound love given and received they are windows for us onto realities beyond time.

Life is teaching me that the Buddha and Kafka and Diogenes were right. Our dogs make us better humans. In the magical realm I call the 'Scottie Crazies' where unconditional love is given and received we practice compassion, tenderness, and generosity uninhibited by the rage and violence in contemporary urban culture. In the domain of the good life with our Scotties noble human impulses are kept alive in a modern desert of incivility.

By contrast to the ephimera of modern hectic living we give our hearts to our Scotties transforming the life we share together into a book of heart-days. That is why to know a Scottie— to really know him and to be known intimately in return— is to write life-pages rich in depth and texture. And I know from experience that to celebrate the old dog whose grey beard is testimonial to heart-days in the scrapbook of communion is to know first hand that the good life does, indeed, begin with a Scottie.

As publisher of *Great Scots Magazine* I have come to believe the future of our breed is in the hands of pet owners. I say this because of sheer numbers and because it is the pet market that subsidizes puppy mills and casual backyard breeding both of which operate outside of long-term understanding of and commitment to the genetic health and vitality of the breed. What Scotties desperately need is informed consumer advocacy commited not merely to individual dogs but to the good of the breed as a whole. Informed, activist Scottie consumers can end irresponsible breeding and promote a healthy Scottie gene pool by simply refusing to purchase puppies from any source, pet store or kennel, which fails to offer proof of knowledgeable, healthful practices and of genetic health-testing. When there are no buyers, there will be no more puppy mill Scotties.

The problem is, how do we foster savvy, responsible pet owners? The answer is not by scolding or shouting mandates but by raising the standard of pet experience through deepening the relational magic between Scotties and their people. When pet owners see their journey with Scotties in its deeper implications they see their dog not as an ornament, but as a partner and teacher who can re-enchant ordinary life through the magic of authentic communion. Such profound inter-species communion changes the way we see Scotties, and the way we see ourselves.

That is the focus of this book— the relational magic between Scotties and their people. My interests go deeper than externalized descriptions of the Scottish Terrier's history and characteristics. What intrigues and motivates me is the inner dynamics, the spiritual journey, reflected in the profound relational 'glue' of the Scottie experience. This book attempts to get inside the passions and commitments of Scottie obsession through the pragmatic voices of ordinary Scottie lovers whose hearts and lives are owned by Scotties. Here is the unaffected language of responsible love for a remarkable breed.

The origin of these chapters is my own pursuit of the Scottie good life— *Great Scots Magazine*. *GSM* is a bi-monthly magazine and personal dream launched in January 1996. It has quickly become an international voice of celebration for Scottish Terrier lovers through its focus on the joy of companionship. This collection from the magazine, selected thematically from the first five years of publication— much of it written by myself as publisher/

editor— offers important value over the original articles because as a collection they achieve thematic depth and continuity impossible in the diffusion of ideas across 28 separately published issues of the magazine. The net effect is powerful amplification of important truths of the Scottie good life.

Part One insists it is the informed Scottie lover who is best able to achieve the good life with these great-souled companions and that to be informed requires understanding of both the breed and of oneself. Part Two is based on the premise that the good life with Scotties is not self-sustaining, that it requires careful nurturing and attention to detail. Scotties are not for those seeking canine yard furniture, but they thrive when bonded to persons willing to take on the responsibilities of relational commitment. Part Three is unique in single breed literature in its grassroots voices celebrating Scottie companionship. Here are unforgettable stories recounting the sunshine of heart-days of joy, and also stories redeeming the shadows of heart-days of grief over the loss of Scottie companions. Whether in sunshine or in shadow, this celebration by Scottie lovers is palpable testimony to the magic of unforgettable dogs.

Scotties are not for everyone. These wee die-hards seek soul-mates, relational partners, and they have their own ideas about the sort of person they prefer to own. Among those devoted to Scotties the vast majority are pet owners whose needs and interests differ from those of breeders. That is why it is important to have the right book to place in the hands of companion seekers contemplating the good life with Scotties— a book which raises the standards of pet ownership by deepening the dynamics of the good life with pets. What is needed is a book written *by* Scottie lovers *for* Scottie lovers which treats compellingly the magic of real companionship in both the sunshine and the shadows which are the package deal of authentic love of Scotties.

It is hoped **The Good Life Begins with a Scottie** is just such a book.

Joseph Harvill,
Publisher/Editor of
Great Scots Magazine

*All chapters without author designation are the work of the Editor. Other writers' works appear under their own bylines.

Part One:
Understanding the Scottie Good Life

"Scotties are Mother Nature's class act."
Joseph Harvill

CHAPTER ONE

The Land and Its Dog

Some observers believe that over time owners and their dogs grow to look alike. I believe this mirroring is true in a far deeper sense than mere physical features. There is correlation also of temperament, mood, and spirit between dogs and their people.

This corrolation is strikingly true in the case of Scotland and her definitive export, the Scottish Terrier. I say definitive export because in manifest ways the Scottie reflects the wonder of Scotland herself.

Scotland was my home for seven years from 1969-1976. Two of my children were born there, and some of my heart is still in the idyllic countryside of Ayrshire near the village of Kilmaurs. During my Scotland years I developed an enduring admiration for the Scottish spirit and for the terrier that to my mind embodies the ethos of the Land of Caledonia. In important ways my life with Scotties has informed and deepened my appreciation of the virtues of their homeland. Reflexively, my awareness of Scotland's history has informed and deepened my understanding of the Scotties I love.

To Scottie lovers our dogs and their ways are familiar, but the story of the Motherland which brought them forth is not. It is my conviction, however, that one cannot fully appreciate Scotties and their spirit unless one sees them against the background of their Scottish origins.

I find at least four definitive parallels between Scotland and her famous terrier, parallels which are keys to appreciating the ethos common to them

Western Highlands of Scotland. Photo by J. Harvill.

both. In these correlations of the dog and its Motherland lie clues for better understanding both the land and its dog.

Parallels of Size

Scotties, like Scotland itself, give the lie to the notion that bigger is better. Both are small yet remarkably large. By North American standards Scotland is tiny. In terms of land mass it's the size of Maine. You could put four Scotlands in my state of New Mexico! Likewise in the canine world Scotties are little guys, standing but 11 inches at the shoulder and weighing around 20 pounds. But the Scottie does not know he is a little guy. Full of piss and vinegar, Scotties have no trace of inferiority. Like their homeland, they are what Aristotle once called "large-souled" beings, in whom size is an attitude and they have more than their share.

That is not surprising when you know that the Scottie's homeland is a place of large-souled people who routinely accomplish great things with little. It is said that in the late 18th century there was more genius on the streets of Edinburgh than could be encountered anywhere on earth. For a small country Scotland has produced more than its share of the great thinkers of the Western world: the ideas of David Hume, Thomas Reid, and John Knox influence philosophy and religion to this day, and native sons Adam Smith, the father of economics, and James Watt, the harnesser of steam power, are arguably the prime shapers of Western industrial culture, inside and out. Scotland is 'big' in other important ways, too. The Scots were first to have a national system of education (1696), and she has great universities older than Columbus' discovery of America: St. Andrews (1411) and Glasgow (1451).

Like the Scotties I have come to know and love Scotland is big despite its size. And the Scottish Terrier, as a big dog in a small package, embodies that paradox perfectly.

Parallels of Loyalty & Affection

Similarly, the Scottish Terrier embodies the loyalty-in-relationships I admire about the Scottish people. Neither Scots nor the terrier that bears their name are generic lovers. Both are selective with their affections and bonding for them is a profound commitment reserved for their special inner circle.

Scotland has always been the epicenter of clans and clan loyalty. Fierce attachment to one's clan is virtually part of Scotland's DNA as self-defense against an almost unbroken history of external exploitation. General Wade's description of Highlanders, written to King George I in 1724, is not only a cameo of the Scottish spirit but also an apposite portrait of the Scottish Terrier:

> " ... their strong friendships, and adherence to those of their own name, tribe and family ... and the little regard they have ever paid to the laws of the Kingdom ... The chiefs of some of these tribes never fail to give countenance and protection to those of their own clan."

In my own experience, the Scots, just like Scottie dogs, do not put on airs or feign friendship with strangers. At first they appear reserved, and some would say, cold. I found it truer to say the Scottish people are neither affected nor superficial, and never fake affection before it is real.

I remember American visitors who came to visit us during our early years in Glasgow who were bewildered by the Scots' non-response to typical Texas-style "Howdys" full of vigorous handshakes and effusive greeting displays. Americans, especially Southerners, tend to smile, posture, and gush during first encounters. Self-respecting Scots do not.

But it is wrong to conclude that Scots are unaffectionate or cold. They are warm and fiercely loyal folks; they simply refuse to trivialize friendship by feining it before it is real. Once formed, however, Scottish relationships are profound and deep and lasting.

Such behavioral description reads like a breed profile to anyone familiar with Scotties: they are generally cordial dogs, but frugal with affections to all but their inner circle. But within the Scottie's primary relational circle there is a depth of bonding that goes beyond what is typically experienced in the pet world. When Scotties love, just like the Scottish people, they love with their whole heart and soul.

It is no accident, therefore, that life with Scottish Terriers mirrors Scottish relationships since Scotties are Scotland's definitive export. Indeed, to know the heartbeat of the Highland Scot is to recognize the pulse of the Scotties we love.

Parallels of Courage

Courage is a second name for Scotties. Called the "die-hard," Scotties are courageous to a fault against all odds.

Where does this come from? Why are Scotties so self-assertive, so territorial, so ready to challenge outsiders? To know Scottish history is to see these terrier traits in a new light.

The story of Scotland is the story of David against Goliath, told over and over again. The threatening 'Goliaths' changed over time but the story of the underdog opposing superior outside forces of domination and exploitation, is the same. The saga begins with conquering Roman legions in the 1st century A.D., and continues later with waves of ferocious invading vikings, and finally the relentless pressure of English domination from south of Scotland's border from the 14th century to the present day. Today since 1970 the story continues in the exploitation of Scotland's resources by foreign interests in the control of North Sea oil.

One especially deplorable chapter in Scotland's struggle against oppression occurred in the late 18th and early 19th centuries— precisely the period of the Scottish Terrier's modern evolution. This chapter was the infamous Highland "clearances." These were wholesale, violent removals of poor Highlanders from their homelands by wealthy land barons to make room first for profitable sheep grazing, then two generations later, to remove the herds and shepherds to make room for profitable deer stalking. Homes were burnt and tens of thousands of men, women, and children were forced to leave at the point of a sword or musket, carrying little or nothing as they were herded to a life of poverty and hunger.

Sadly, Scotland's 'David and Goliath' tale does not share the miraculous ending of the biblical narrative. Too often the story of Scotland is the sad tale of the little guy paying in blood the price for resisting superior force.

But resist they always have. Against all odds, despite outcomes, the Scots always have been the original 'die-

Sterling Castle near which occurred the Battle of Bannockburn, where Robert the Bruce led the Scots against the English.

hards.' Today when you visit the north of England and the border country between England and Scotland you still can see vestiges of Hadrian's Wall which dates to c. A.D. 120 marking the northern-most border of the ancient Roman Empire in Britain. The invaders from Italy conquered England but gave up on subduing the feisty Scots and built a wall to protect themselves. To this day that wall's remnants stand as testament to the fiercely courageous spirit of Scotland.

And that is my point with reference to Scotties: anyone who has been owned by a Scottie knows well this same courageous spirit. This trait of character in our dogs is not an accident of Nature, nor was our breed created in a vacuum. These die-hard traits we prize in our dogs did not just happen, they are the product of human engineering and choice by the Highlanders who were the architects of our breed and who left marks of their own spirit and values embedded in the genes of the terrier they created. In my experience, to know intimately the Scottie temperament is to trace close and small the history of courage which is Scotland.

Parallels of Independence

The fourth manifestation of parallels between the land and its dog is our breed's inveterate independence. Scotties are "free thinkers" and stubbornly self-directed.

Some breeds can be banned from the couch and they accept it as off limits. A Scottie, however, will think about the ban and probably ignore it— at least while you are out of the room. To him it makes no sense why a location prized by his Person should be prohibited to him. They are strong-willed, and the success or failure of Scottie companionship is largely a matter of coming to terms relationally with their strong sense of themselves and their stubborn independence, traits which are both their joy and their exasperation.

Once again I am saying this trait of stubborn, 'free-thinking' independence is best understood against the background of the independent Scots whose spirit is mirrored in the breed they created in the Highlands of Scotland. That spirit is best personified in the Scottish Empiricist thinker David Hume (1711-1776), who has had profound impact on Western philosophy, echoes of whose voice are overheard daily at universities from Berkeley to Oxford. His *Treatise of Human Nature* and his ideas regarding causality and moral reason will likely continue to define philosophical debate in the 21st century.

My argument is not that our Scotties are wee Scottish philosophers—although a case might be made for it! What I am arguing is that the cultural ethos and spirit which gave birth to David Hume's independent thinking is the same fiercely independent ethos and spirit that bred the Scottish Terrier we know and love. The independent spirit of the Motherland is replicated close and small in the terrier that bears her name.

Conclusion

I realize there are problems anthropomorphizing our dogs, i.e., attributing to them human characteristics. I know Scotties are canines, not human beings, and that they are descendants of the wolf, not 'fur-people.' I know.

I know also that nothing occurs devoid of context without a 'before' and 'after' the understanding of which is essential to any clear interpretation of meaning. Scotties originated, not out of the blue, but in a particular place at a point in space and time, and I believe that particularity is manifest in their nature. The traits we prize in our dogs are triumphs of genetic engineering by Highland Scots who knew little about genetics but everything about loyalty, courage, and independence. The spirit and values of highland mountain and glen are embodied in the terrier they created. To know the spirit of that time and place is to grasp the spirit of the Scottie that originated there.

So for me the Scottish Terrier is much more than a wee black dog. When I look at my Scotties I see Scotland's definitive export because these little Scotsmen embody the large-souled spirit of Scotland herself.

> *This is my country*
> *The land that begat me.*
> *These windy spaces*
> *Are surely my own.*
> *And those who here toil*
> *In the sweat of their faces*
> *Are flesh of my flesh,*
> *And bone of my bone.*
> Sir Alexander Gray

Further Reading

"The Land & Its Dog" is a revised version of *"Scotland's Definitive Export: The Scottish Terrier,"* by Joseph Harvill, Ph.D., which first appeared in *GSM Vol 1 No 5 (Sep/Oct) 1996.*

For the 'orthodox' history of Scotland see J.D. Mackie, *A History of Scotland*. NY: Penguin Books, 1991, 414 pp. A less orthodox, but deeply passionate history from a Scots nationalist point of view is Rex Welldon Finn, M.A., *Scottish Heritage*. London: William Heinemann LTD, 1938, 297 pp. Finn's account of the "clearances" is partisan and compelling.

For more on the Highland Clearances and Scotland today see the website of *Highlander Web Magazine* @ *http://www.catalyst-highlands.co.uk*

The best sources for the early background history of the Scottish Terrier are: D.J. Thomson Gray, *The Dogs of Scotland: Their Varieties, History, Characteristics, and Exhibition Points*. James P. Mathew, Edinburgh, 1891; Fayette C. Ewing, M.D., *The Book of the Scottish Terrier*. NY: Orange Judd Publishing Co, 1932; Dr. William A. Bruette, *The Scottish Terrier*. NY: G. Howard Watt, 1934.

CHAPTER TWO

The Scottie M.Y.S.T.I.Q.U.E.

Cindy Cooke, author of **The New Scottish Terrier** (1996), says it is the character of the Scottish Terrier which charms and captivates. She also says an adequate description of that unique character is a daunting challenge. As she puts it, Scottie lovers find themselves *"grasping for metaphors to describe the breed that has stolen their hearts."*

She is right. Not merely because metaphors are challenging, but because appraisals are reflexive, blurring the line between subject and object. Scottie mystique has more to do with what is *between* Scotties and their people than with hard data of breed demographics, and therefore, accounts of Scottie character tell as much about ourselves, our experience, and our values as about the dog described.

There is no need to apologize for that. There simply is no other way to appraise soul and character than by reference to metaphors and one's own lights.

That said, what can we say of the Scottie mystique? Shunning illusions of exhaustive truth, what metaphors can we enlist to provide at least keyhole glimpses of what I call the *scottie-ness* of a Scottie?

A useful framework for such an analysis of Scottie mystique is an acronym made up of the letters in the word *mystique* itself. For this Scottie lover at least, the word *mystique* and its meaning, together with relational memories I attach to the individual letters, add up to a robust notion of what is special about the character of the Scottish Terrier.

'M' For Mystery

'M' is for the *mystery* at the heart of the Scottie mystique. Perhaps the first thing one notices about a Scottie in public is an unmistakable air of "I-am-special-and-don't-you-know-it." It is a combination of dignity, self-assurance, and poise, and at times suggests to me almost a self-aware burden of greatness. It is the mystique of the Scottie!

The word mystique is French, and connotes "an air or attitude of mystery and reverence developing around something or someone; the special esoteric skill essential in a calling or activity."

Scotties exude mystique. It is recognizable in the well-known "Scottie walk," as well as in their imperious manner in relationships. It is as if the Scottie's destiny were to be Mother Nature's class act— and their soul evolved knowing it!

My own sense is there is mystery in the soul of the Scottie. Mystery in the sense that he always holds something back, has something more in reserve. What you encounter is not all there is. Much like a person, the Scottie spirit is complex, and it is the hidden 'something more' which one suspects is definitive.

You catch glimpses of this mystery at the heart of the Scottie when you watch him unawares as he enjoys his own company, as he surveys his world through window or gate, or as he sits in solitude apparently pondering life's imponderables. Sometimes you encounter the mystery in his eyes when you catch him thoughtfully studying you, and in the eye contact which follows there are astonishing glimpses of something deep and profound within.

Scotties can be aloof and psychologically distant. They can earn their reputation as "snotty scottie." But to those who know them there is more than canine egoism at their center. There is facinating mystery and mystique which keeps us coming back for more!

'Y' For Yesterday

More so than many breeds the Scottie's history is written in his heart and form. To know the Scottie's character one must know his *yesterdays*.

To know his role as vermin exterminator in the rugged Western Highlands of Scotland is to appreciate at a glance the marvel of design embodied in his dense, wiry coat; in his short, muscled limbs, large head and over-sized teeth; in his independent spirit, and tenacious, die-hard resolve. In the cairns and dens of Highland vermin burrows the timid do not survive and the co-dependent do not succeed.

In a singular sense the land and the dog are one. To walk Highland glens and moors, at once both friendly and fierce, and to meet the bruised but proud spirit of the Highlander is to see with new eyes the dog that wears Scotland's name. To read with sympathy the David-against-Goliath history of Scotland's defiant battles against foreign domination is to glimpse the soul of the "diehard."

In special ways, to know Scottie's 'yesterday' is to know more than dry history. It is to understand his mystique.

'S' For Sagacity

The Scottie is a *sage* and philosopher among canines.

The notion of Scotties as philosophers is not as silly as it sounds. No less a philosopher than Plato paid tribute to dogs as model teachers of a life of wisdom. In ***The Republic***, Book II, Socrates ponders how it is "That the sight of an unknown person angers (a dog) before he has suffered any injury, but an acquaintance he will fawn upon though he has never received any kindness from him." Socrates, somewhat tongue-in-cheek, argues a dog's grounds for such discrimination between friend and alien is knowledge and/or ignorance, and that such a trait of nature "shows a true love of wisdom" in their habit of grounding responses in knowledge.

I find Plato's language true to experience, and not ironical. Scotties are 'thinking' dogs in a sense quite remarkable. As novelist and champion Scottie-breeder, S.S. Van Dine, wrote in 1932:

"[The Scottie] is one of the few dogs with whom human beings can actually argue. Scotties have their own ideas about things-- they work out their problems and arrive at very definite conclusions-- and they will go to the mat with you on any issue. If you are right they will, in the end, give in; but if you are wrong from their canine point of view (which, incidentally, is a highly sensible one), they can be as stubborn as only a Scotchman (*sic*) can be ... but they have that aristocratic and gentlemanly instinct which somehow makes them see when they are wrong; and, like a gentleman, they will acquiesce graciously when the truth is brought home to them."

The Scottie as thinker has little to do with parlor tricks or stimulus-response training. Dog trainers who demonstrate prowess in canine intelligence by showing off with sheep dogs stack the deck in their own favor by choosing canines with mind-control in their DNA. Scotties, on the other hand, were bred to think and act on their own in isolated and dangerous sub-terranean situations where external directives and control did not exist. Underground, facing ferocious teeth and defenses of a trapped predator, one thinks quickly and independently or one does not survive!

As the Scottie matures he wears the role of thinking dog ever more adeptly. Study his face in his solitude. You will see modeled what Plato was referring to when he spoke of dogs as true "lovers of wisdom," and what I mean when I speak of Scottie 'sagacity.'

'T' For Terrier

"T" in the Scottie mystique stands for *terrier*. First to last, from beginning to end, the Scottie is the quintessential terrier.

'Terrier' comes from the Latin word for 'earth' and points to 'earth dog' origins and the Scottie's primal function of going-to-ground in pursuit of prey. Originally one of a number of "lurcher" dogs, it was the Scottie's task to enter the burrows and sanctuaries of the fox and wildcat, to flush them out or fight them underground to the death. Gameness, without reference to size or circumstance, was and is the heart of the terrier.

That is why Scotties are fearless when challenged. Size is an attitude with them, and the Scottie has more than his share! They are ideal watchdogs, since it is noise which primarily deters thieves. The intensity of the terrier spirit renders Scotties constantly vigilant against intruders, and their larger-than-life bark sounds an alarm which cannot be ignored. On the other hand, Scottie terrier-ness makes them ill-suited to be doormats or yard ornaments. Their terrier-spirit is too high-strung and their self-awareness too developed to allow anything less than a peer relationship. Some may find this spirit of canine egality a nuisance. I find in it the soul of the Scottie mystique.

'I' For Independent

Scotties are *independent* wee dogs, quite capable of enjoying their own company. More cat-like than many breeds, Scotties often appear to want affection strictly on their terms. That is not to say there are no lap dogs among Scotties, but it is to say that a remarkable independence of spirit is trademark of the breed.

Some find such independence unwelcome. To them it is stubbornness and a threat to their own control. Pets, after all, are to be subservient and docile, an extension of the will of their masters.

By contrast, I find my Scotties refuse to be clones of my will, they challenge my self-absorption, and they confront me with the reality of *Other-ness*. In my better moments, when I permit myself to get beyond struggles of will, I discover in our conflicts and in their eyes the mystery of self-awareness in beings other than humans. To crush that independence or to co-opt it as extension of myself is to lose the gift of authentic encounter with non-human others.

Scottie independence can be exasperating, to be sure. It also enables Scotties to be experienced, not as clones, but as authentic relational partners.

'Q' For Quixotic

Quixotic is the substantive describing the ethos and spirit of Don Quixote, the man from la Mancha. In the Cervantes novel, Don Quixote personifies one who is "foolishly impractical especially in the pursuit of ideals." In the story, Quixote, against all odds, risks all to fight the impossible foe and to dream the impossible dream.

That story and the word *quixotic* might have been written about the diehard spirit of the Scottish Terrier. The best description of the Scottie as a canine Quixote-figure is that of S.S. Van Dine, written in 1932:

"[The Scottie] meets life as he finds it, with an instinctive philosophy, a stoical intrepidity and a mellow understanding. He is calm and firm, and he minds his own business— and minds it well. He is a Spartan and can suffer pain without whimpering— which is more than the majority of human beings can do. He will attack a lion or a tiger if his rights are invaded, and though he may die in the struggle he never shows the white feather or runs away. He is the most admirable of all sports-- forthright, brave and uncomplaining. You know exactly where you stand with a Scottie; and if you are a friend, he is gentle, loving and protective."

In our age of ethics by poll tabulation and truth by spin-doctoring there is something welcome and real about the Scottie spirit of quixotic integrity against all odds. I find it an inspiring aspect of the Scottie mystique.

'U' For Unique

From his shape to his spirit, the Scottie is *unique*. Out walking, the Scottie will be recognized by passers-by who normally would not distinguish a Beagle from a Bichon. *"Oh, look. There goes a Scottie!"* is the typical exclamation overheard from young and old alike when we walk our three in public.

It is true, of course, that Scotties have no monopoly on dog love. But it is also true that Scottie love is distinctive. I say that because no other Whitehouse canine ever captured the imagination of the American public as did Roosevelt's Scottie, Fala, nor does any other breed have its own national organization of collectors— some of whom do not own Scottie dogs— dedicated to collecting everything sporting a Scottie, ranging from furniture to figurines. The sheer quantity of such collectibles is unique, no other breed coming close to inspiring the quantity and range of collectibles bearing its effigy. Furthermore, no other breed is recognizable by name to non-dog people quite like the Scottish Terrier. Scotties and Scottie love are in a category by themselves.

Therefore I say the Scottish Terrier is unique in ways both external and internal. To those up to the challenge, the Scottie's uniqueness offers canine companionship which knows no equal.

'E' For Esquire

In British parlance *'esquire'* is a member of the English gentry ranking below a knight, or, historically, a candidate for knighthood serving as shield bearer and attendant to a knight. Today, abbreviated as 'Esq.' it is a British title of courtesy, short for something like "gentleman-of-good-standing."

I have always felt there is something genteel about the Scottie's bearing, something of the well-bred gentleman in his manner. And the picture of shield bearer who puts himself in harm's way loyally attending to the safety of his knight vividly portrays the protective spirit of the Scottie. To me the word gentleman or lady best describes the mature Scottie. As Dorothy Gabriel wrote long ago:

"There is nothing frothy or shallow in the nature of the Scottie. He never forgets-- his heart may break with grief, but he will not yowl about it. He is absolutely honorable, incapable of a mean or petty action, large hearted and loving, with the soul and mind of an honest gentleman."

Today something is sadly lost from the language of that kinder, gentler era when 'gentleman' designated quality of soul and manners, not mere gender. The word 'gentleman,' however, still captures the soul and manners of the Scottie at his best. He has class. And that is why for this Scottie lover 'e' in the Scottie *mystique* stands for Scottish Terrier, *Esq*.

Conclusion

So there you have it—one man's vision of the Scottie mystique. I know to some, all of it is hopeless sentimentalism. To which I say, I would not have it any other way. For it is habits of the heart which define us as human beings and I know my habits of heart have been greatly enriched by the love of Scotties.

I could mention many personal encounters which illustrate what I have attempted to say. I think of my three, Nati, Gus, and Willie, so different in personality yet so focused in their love and loyalty, and they form for me what St. Paul once called "living epistles" in which I daily read new truths of the Scottie mystique.

One special experience says it all. It is the image of Gus in my peripheral vision as I sit at the computer in my office. He has entered the room unawares and silently raises himself onto his haunches, statue-like, forepaws raised in supplication as he waits motionless to make eye contact with the man he loves. Dark eyes speaking volumes, he waits without sound for me to notice him and to respond. No one taught him this entreaty. Nor do the other two Scotties employ it. It is his own chosen form of communication with the one he loves. Sometimes he supplicates to be let outdoors. More often his supplication simply is to be lifted up onto my lap, forepaws on my shoulders, for a hug and gentle conversation. What does it all mean? Simply this: "Master, I love you!"

Yet Gus never had churches, nor schools, nor legislatures to teach him the one thing most needful for the good life; no professors to give him knowledge; no lawyers to define his ethics, and yet he is educated beyond them all, as if to say: "Master, am I not already educated, do I not know how to love?"

Yes, Gus, true gentleman, you do indeed know how to love. And that knowledge is the miracle of your kind and your great gift to life.

Further Reading

"The Scottie M.Y.S.T.I.Q.U.E." is a revised version of *"Defining the Scottie M.Y.S.T.I.Q.U.E.,"* by Joseph Harvill, Ph.D., which first appeared in *GSM* Vol 3 No 6 (Nov/Dec) 1998.

Cindy Cooke, *The New Scottish Terrier*. NY: Howell Book House, 1996.

Dorothy Gabriel, ***The Scottish Terrier: Its Breeding and Management***. London: The Dog World, LTD., n.d. (c. 1932).

The Republic of Plato, trans., with an Introduction by A.D. Lindsay, NY: E.P. Dutton, 1957.

S.S. Van Dine quotes and much more on the Scottish Terrier can be found in Fayette C. Ewing, M.D.; F.A.C.S., ***The Book of the Scottish Terrier***. NY: Orange Judd Pub. Co., 1946.

The dog pictured this page is Aylser of Allascot, "Meg," bred by Doreen Blackstone, Stamford, England.

CHAPTER THREE

Good Dogs Are Made Not Born

It is a fact of life that many dogs of all breeds have no manners. More to the point, because Scotties often are indulged and pampered they can become ill-mannered offenders. Sadly, such Scotties are why our breed is stereotyped by outsiders as barkers or biters or as stubborn and untrainable.

An example of such stereotyping is Jane Brody's recent New York Times popularization of the Scottie-bashing published by B.L. and L.A. Hart in their book, *The Perfect Puppy*. The book reports rankings by 96 dog experts of the 56 most common purebred dogs in 13 socialization categories. In categories of 'excitability,' 'snapping at children,' 'barking,' 'aggression,' and 'dominance over owner,' the Scottie is among the top 10 percent of offenders, and in the category of 'trainability' Scotties are ranked in the bottom third of breeds!

Clearly such broadbrush stereotyping of the Scottish Terrier is both inaccurate and offensive to those of us who know and love the breed. Beyond quarreling with this or that conclusion from these authors' rankings, Scottie lovers feel inclined to counter that Scottie pluck and spirit is central to their charm and that if high spirited dogs are judged 'imperfect' for some humans that fact tells as much about the humans as about the dog.

The purpose here, however, is not to spar with Brody or the Harts, but to make three points for Scottie lovers: first, to draw attention to common negative perceptions of Scotties; second, to make the point that good dogs, whether

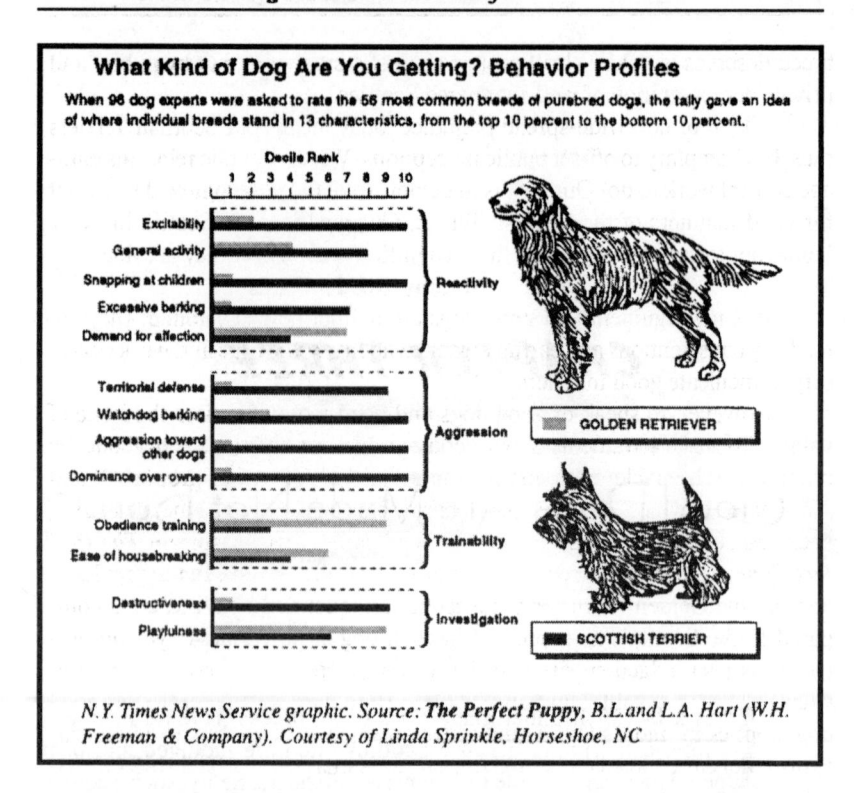

What Kind of Dog Are You Getting? Behavior Profiles

When 96 dog experts were asked to rate the 56 most common breeds of purebred dogs, the tally gave an idea of where individual breeds stand in 13 characteristics, from the top 10 percent to the bottom 10 percent.

Reactivity: Excitability, General activity, Snapping at children, Excessive barking, Demand for affection

Aggression: Territorial defense, Watchdog barking, Aggression toward other dogs, Dominance over owner

Trainability: Obedience training, Ease of housebreaking

Investigation: Destructiveness, Playfulness

GOLDEN RETRIEVER

SCOTTISH TERRIER

N.Y. Times News Service graphic. Source: **The Perfect Puppy**, *B.L. and L.A. Hart (W.H. Freeman & Company). Courtesy of Linda Sprinkle, Horseshoe, NC*

Scotties or any other breed, are made, not born; and third, to highlight my theme that Scottie manners are the responsibility of Scottie owners.

Negative Perceptions

The fact that knowledgeable dog people look askance at our breed should motivate us to a new sense of accountability as owners. Protecting our breed from exploitation by puppy mills is on every Scottie lover's mind. Unfortunately, it never occurs to some who would fight tooth and nail to eradicate puppy mills that neglect of proper socialization and training promulgates a bad dog image for our breed and that this is its own form of breed abuse. Bad mannered Scotties do more than inflame critics; they rob our dogs of dignity and respect, and more important, bad manners rob our dogs of higher levels of bonding and companionship at home.

The only Scotties some people will ever know are your dogs. Since you and your dogs leave an impression on every person you meet, and since that impression may be positive or negative, a mental picture of our breed will linger in observer's minds based on the behavior seen or unseen in your Scottie. That is why you and your dog must take seriously your role as ambassadors. My point is, the way to silence breed critics and to earn the respect our breed deserves is not by shrill protest against stereotyping but by public and private demonstration of well-mannered Scotties.

Like it or not, wide-spread prejudice today means our Scottish Terriers must be exemplary to off-set public perceptions. We have public relations damage control work to do! Our task is to demonstrate the unrecognized potential for good manners of the Scottish Terrier. Our goal is not a Scottie in every home, but to earn for our breed the recognition and respect they are due.

Making Good

It is my argument that good dogs are neither born nor found; they are made by conscientious and caring owners who invest the time and work necessary to inculcate good manners.

However, to speak of good dogs and good manners raises the issue of values. To make judgments about good and bad we must be clear about the criteria which enable us to answer the questions, "On what grounds?" and "Compared to what?" Criteria matter because when you change the measuring stick you change the measure. You see an example of such a shift in *The Perfect Puppy* research referred to earlier (see illustration p. 26). In the graphic it appears the Golden Retriever's 'investigation' quotient is judged good compared to the Scottie's as expressed in each dog's 'playfulness,' yet the Retriever is also judged superior to the Scottie in 'reactivity' because the Retriever is less 'excitable' and less 'active.' Here the implied verdict of 'good dog' applies to 'more playful' and simultaneously to 'less active.' These categories appear contradictory, and one suspects unacknowledged shifts in criteria at work in the evaluations.

Herein lies some of the problem in regard to defining 'good' Scotties. Companionship criteria for the good dog can be quite different from showring values. Whereas managed aggression in the showring exhibited as "sparing" may win points with dogshow judges, aggressive behavior will not win friends on neighborhood walks. Toilet training is scarcely an issue for kenneled dogs, but it directly impacts the quality of life for the companion dog.

So what is a good Scottie? Let me be explicit about my values. My criteria have everything to do with companionship and life-long bonds between Scotties and their people, and little to do with breed standards for champions. For my purposes here the good Scottie is the dog whose socialized behavior not only fits his human family's values but also whose good manners promote family harmony. Such a dog might not be considered a good dog in the showring, and conversely the showring stud might not be a good dog in my sense. When speaking of the good life intimately shared, matters of the heart and hearth are the criteria that count.

So what are the heart and hearth criteria? Minimum standards for the good Scottie would include the following:

- Comes when called
- Obeys 'sit' command
- Obeys 'stay' command
- No biter
- Friendly to guests, human and animal
- Bark control
- Bladder/bowel control
- Chew and dig control
- Walk etiquette

Other criteria could be included, but these are baselines, since lack of these good manners spoils the quality of life a Scottie shares with his Persons. These nine basics are not excessive and they are within the reach of every Scottie owner. Our problem typically is not that our Scotties are incorrigible nor that we are incapable, but merely that we are lazy or lack the will to actualize change.

Make no mistake. There is work in making good dogs, just as there is work in quality child-rearing. Scotties are not born well-mannered any more than are children. Being civil, friendly, and trustworthy is the outgrowth of good behaviors taught, rewarded, and reinforced— over, and over, and over again.

Scottie World

"It's always 'Sit!' 'Stay!' 'Heel!'— never 'Think,' 'Innovate!' 'Follow your bliss!'"

The problem facing Scotties and all breeds today is not that they are bad dogs but that they are assimilating into a human culture in jeopardy of losing its own sense of manners and civility. Today's pets are ill-mannered because the humans in charge are rapidly becoming mannerless.

So here is another of those reflexive links between ourselves and our Scotties through which bettering our dogs becomes a mirror for upgrading ourselves. Taking seriously our Scotties' needs for discipline and manners can stimulate us to recognize the need for new grace notes in our own conduct, and in doing so, the trainers are themselves trained in the art of living more nobly.

Good Owners

To put a fine point on it, I am arguing it is not bad Scotties which is our problem; it is bad owners. Owners make Scotties good and it is owners who make bad ones.

There are many excuses why we fail to effectively socialize our dogs: too little time, timidity, and even false notions that discipline and training quash the Scottie personality. This last notion about quashing the Scottie spirit highlights important truth regarding the rationale for all our dog training. Worry over warping our Scottie's personality is a vestige of wooly-headed Spockian-psychology of the 1960s which crippled human parenting by severing esteem from accountability. By contrast, the holistic perspective of Systems Theory makes plain that neither our Scotties nor ourselves can behave without consequences since we are connected and what affects one impacts all in the system.

This is the truth which inspires all current ecology thinking, and here is the important rationale for responsible Scottie making. *Our dogs are part of our human 'sub-systems' and therefore fitting compatibly into those systems is vital to everyone's health and happiness.*

The hard fact is it is *our* human world, not the world of the wild kingdom, that is the system into which our Scotties must merge and contribute. This system is alien and unnatural from the canine perspective, and filled with non-sense realities as well as life-threatening dangers from speeding cars to poisons. Therefore fitting in successfully is not a luxury; their lives depend on it. Furthermore, it is *our* choice to assimilate Scotties into our system, not theirs. Because it is *our* world and *our* arbitrary choice, it is *our* responsibility to equip our dogs to be harmonious members of the system. Banning or giving up on them because training turns out to be neither quick nor easy is sheer irresponsibility.

I believe our Scotties want to fit in because by nature they are pack animals and that means it is their canine nature to be social creatures. But our human world with its rules and ambiguities is not theirs by nature, so they rely on us to teach them how to fit in. When we train them and teach them good manners we are 'humanizing' them in order that their natural dogishness can adapt in our world where they are infinitely vulnerable. Such 'humanizing' is neither cruel nor heartless; it is the loving way to insure their prosperity. Abdication of this human responsibility to teach and to train is the number one cause for the crisis-intervention of Scottie Rescue. The truth is, when you bring a dog into your human world, to love that Scottie is to train it. To do less is to fail your own best self and to jeopardize the dog and its future.

Homemade Good

So where to begin? How do you make your own homemade good dogs?

The place to begin is with a fuller understanding of bonding. Technically, this is not training at all, yet without it training is doomed. When you and your Scottie know the magic of emotional connection, that bond forms the powerful ground for both training and obedience. When bonded, commands and corrections are benevolent and obedience is willing.

This area of emotional attachment is where Scotties and their people shine. Our dogs are more likely to suffer from indulgence than from abuse. Because we typically dote on them our Scotties frequently eat a healthier diet and receive better medical care than we give ourselves! All this attachment can be a plus in training since it provides the basis for success. What is lacking for most of us is the recognition that just as we would not think of jeopardizing our Scotties' health by denying them medical attention, so also when we love our dogs we cannot leave them at risk socially by denying them the rich enhancement which training brings to their lives shared with humans.

In addition to understanding the role of bonding, the next big step is commiting to training. Like human education, Scottie learning is best when it is life-learning, that is, not only a real part of everyday life, but a process that continues throughout life. If you do not really believe training is vital to you and to your Scottie, you probably will not have the stamina to stay with it.

By commiting to training I include every form of structured learning by which you change behavior and gain on-going control over your Scottie in the basic categories of obedience listed earlier. It is the end result—the control—that is vital here, not how you get there. Whether formal training courses or private instruction or both in combination, the serendipity from training and shared life-learning is the making of memories together and deepened bonds of companionship.

Scottie World

The next step is to educate yourself that learning is growth, and to set reasonable expectations. Both you and your Scottie are learning each other's 'foreign' language and that makes communication difficult, especially at first. Initially, all language acquisition seems im-

Feeling a bit squirrely tonight, are we?

possible and non-native speakers despair of ever gaining true fluency. But learning to understand and to speak another's language is not impossible. Difficult, yes, but not impossible. It is helpful to remember as you struggle to get your Scottie to understand what you want her to do that you are facing not only an initial 'language' barrier; you are trying to bridge a species barrier. On the positive side you and your Scottie do not have to rush. Mutual understanding is not a race; the ultimate goal of communication is not speed. You are after a deep and lasting behavioral learning, not a superficial fix. So take your time; be patient and persistent. The rewards in mutual respect and love and the shared good life are worth it!

In terms of actual instruction you require training as well as your Scottie. My recommendation is that you seek out a competent professional and enroll in a formal obedience-training course in your hometown. The purpose of obedience schools is not so much to teach your dog as it is to teach *you* how to teach your dog. Such courses teach you 'dog-lish,' the language canines understand, and that is the language in which you want to become fluent. The American Kennel Club will send you a *'Geographical List of AKC Show and Obedience Clubs'* so you can locate the nearest credentialed program. Contact: ***The American Kennel Club***, 5580 Centerview Dr., Suite #200, Raleigh, NC 27606. Phone: (919) 233-9767. Also, ask about their *'Canine Good Citizen Program.'*

Conclusion

Good dogs are made, not born. Because of the rich benefits to companionship good dogs are worth every bit of work it takes to develop them. Training raises your Scottie's security in a dangerous human world, it provides important cognitive challenge to you and your dog, it fosters higher-level bonding, and it nourishes relational happiness and fulfillment.

Raising a well-mannered Scottie is a challenge, to be sure, but it is the best companionship investment you will ever make. In terms of heart-days you will share with your dog, you can say "No train; no gain." To truly love a Scottie is to want the best for her and that means bonded love revelling in good manners and mutual respect.

Further Reading

This chapter is a revised version of *'Good Dogs Are Made Not Born,'* by Joseph Harvill, which first appeared in ***Great Scots Magazine***, Vol 2 No1 (Jan/Feb, 1997).

On this theme see: Jeanne Carlson with Ranny Green, ***Good Dogs, Bad Habits: The Complete A-to-Z Guide for Solving Your Dog's Behavior Problems***. NY: Fireside Books, 1995.

Jack Volhard and Melissa Bartlett, ***What All Good Dogs Should Know: The Sensible Way to Train***. NY: Howell Book House, 1991.

CHAPTER FOUR

The Scottie Crazies and the Ties That Bind

There is a curious phenomenon I call the "Scottie Crazies." You know what I mean. Poke a Scottie person anywhere and out comes stories and photos and superlatives. Whereas other breed owners with the 'crazies' stand out as exceptions, for Scotties it's the rule. Scottie folks typically have multiple Scotties, we hoard Scottie collectibles, and we wear and breathe expressions of our Scottie love. There is a profound relational glue between us that we feel sets us and our dogs apart. As one die-hard exclaimed to me, "I get excited over my Scotties, not my grandchildren!"

Call it "Scottie Crazies" or whatever, there is a relational magic here worth celebrating. It is deep. It is profound. It is real. To us the good life cannot be defined apart from our Scottie companions.

It is precisely this magic, this enriching bond of companionship between Scotties and their people that I have made the focus of ***Great Scots Magazine***. But how can we nurture that magic? How can we enhance our experience of Scottie companionship so we insure for ourselves and our Scotties our optimal good life together?

Clues

As a first step toward enhancing our Scottie companionship we can locate important clues to success from research into human interpersonal communication. In other words, we can learn a great deal about the ingredients of the good life shared with our Scotties by looking closely at the ingredients of the good life enjoyed by successful human companions.

It is my belief that companionship, whether among humans or interspecies companionship between humans and Scotties, is nurtured and enhanced by similar investments. Like any other relationship, you get out of your Scottie relationship according to what you put into it. And like computer programming, your relationship with your Scottie is a 'G.I.G.O.' situation: "garbage in; garbage out." On the other hand, when you nurture your Scottie relationships with quality investments of time and soul, you multiply your relational joy a hundred fold.

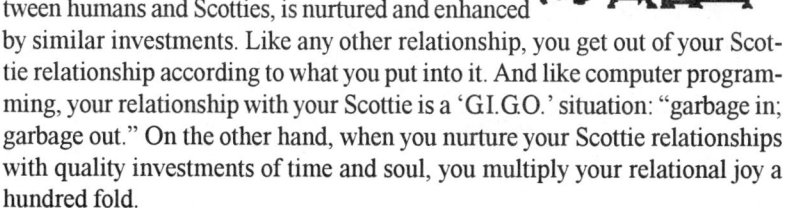

Drawing, then, on the findings of human communication researchers, let me sum up and apply to our Scottie relationships some elements of relational success.

New Perspective

The first key to a deeper relationship with your Scottie is a new perspective. My message here is that just like human relationships, what Scottie lovers treasure as 'special' is not located in the dog, *per se*, nor in the human partner, but in what Scotties and their people have between them.

This concept of 'betweenness' is the discovery of interpersonal communication scholar John Stewart, of the University of Washington, and is important for owner/dog relationships as well as for human pairs because it orients us toward neither the dog in isolation nor ourselves alone, but rather toward the synergy between two unique spirits. Synergy means that together you are greater than the sum of your separate capacities. It means that there is the potential in your communion for you and your Scotties to so interact as to mutually stretch your individual potential.

This is not absurd. I believe strongly that a properly nurtured Scottie relationship makes human partners better people, and makes Scotties better dogs. I also believe that on the whole, in the matter of human-canine getting and giving, humans do more getting than giving, and that we compound the inequity by taking for granted the Scottie angels who minister in our lives!

Such 'betweenness' perspective as Stewart and others advocate for optimal human relationships offers at least one area of special benefit for our Scottie companionship. It reminds us that discipline problems are not isolable in the dog, nor in the human, but lie 'between' Scotties and their people. In other words, I am a partner in both the problem as well as the solution. I am not the enemy, nor is the enemy my dog. The 'mess' is what is 'between' us.

With this new perspective on relationships you can approach problem-solving in a whole new spirit. You and your dog are allies, not opponents, in tackling your shared problem. By recognizing that the problem is located in the relational undergrowth, in the mess 'between' you, you avoid demonizing your dog or yourself. Additionally, by externalizing rather than internalizing your problems you channel energy into joint-solutions instead of blame and recrimination.

Making Memories

The second key to deeper companionship with Scotties is recognition of the importance of shared history. Deep relationships take time, and this is as true of relations with our dogs as with humans.

But the time to which I refer here encompasses more than accumulation of days, weeks, and years. This shared history has more to do with the heart than with the calendar. My mother used to say life is about making memories. She was right. And the deepest memories are always heart matters redolent with emotional color.

This means one of the key ways you can enrich your Scottie companionship is to actively make memories with your dog. Your memories may be of trips together, or birthday parties, or regular walks. They may be of competitions lost and won, or of crises endured together. There are as many different ways to make memories as there are minds to remember.

But in making memories there are two important *musts*: (1) make them matters of the heart, i.e., forget what the neighbors might think, do what you and your Scottie love most, *chase your passion*; (2) do not just *intend* to make memories, do it today! In my kitchen hangs a quotation of wisdom for life from an 85 year-old senior who was asked what he would do if he had his life to live over. He said:

"... I'd try to make more mistakes next time. I would relax ... I would be sillier than I have been this trip. I know of a very few things I would take seriously ... I would have more actual troubles and fewer imaginary ones. You see, I am one of those people who lives prophylactically and sensibly and sanely hour after hour, day after day. Oh, I've had my moments; and if I had it to do over again, I'd have more of them. In fact, I'd try to have nothing else. Just moments, one after another, instead of living so many years ahead each day ... If I had it to do over again, I would go places, do things, and travel lighter than I have ... I would ride on more merry-go-rounds and pick more daisies."

Some day your only regrets will be the memories you did not make.

Commitment

The third key to relational magic is old-fashioned commitment.

I realize this term has fallen out of fashion in recent years. Like all else in our consumer culture, relationships have become disposable. By contrast, the quality of your Scottie companionship will likely depend on your resolute will to commit "for better or for worse." This is especially true during the period after the honeymoon infatuation has worn off your new Scottie puppy. I recall vividly my horror years ago when I discovered my expensive graduate school books mangled by Scottie puppy teeth. And our personal household experience confirms Murphy's (Scottie Puppy) Law: when your pup elects a shoe to destroy, out of multiple options, the one trashed will be the most expensive!

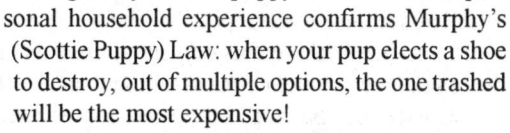

The truth is when you bring your new dog home the fantasy ends and the work begins. It can be expensive, exhausting, and exasperating. And, like a new baby, it's every day. What is more, it is not only the new Scottie that brings trials. Veterinary bills can be crippling for owners of older Scotties, or those facing allergy battles or life-threatening disease.

I say this not to ignore the pleasures of Scottie ownership but to affirm the responsibilities of companionship. The world is too lonely a place ever to trivialize companionship by taking it for granted. The price of knowing firsthand the magic of being owned by a Scottie is forever commitment. No prenuptial loop holes here. No as-long-as-it-is-convenient clauses. Our relational bonds will be deepest and our rewards greatest when our commitment mirrors that of our loyal Scotties and is without reservation.

Communication

The fourth key to deepening your Scottie companionship is effective communication.

There is more here than a truism. Just like human relationships, bonding between Scotties and their people is nurtured by good communication. The trouble is, not all communication is good and it is not true that more communication is always better. More nagging, for instance, is still nagging, and is a poor basis for communion. That goes for people as well as for pets. Likewise less communication can be *more*, if the 'less' refers to communication that authentically conveys affirmation, caring, and attachment in place of a surfeit of talk which is insincere or negative.

I advocate talking to your Scottie, even singing to them, taking care to frequently verbalize their name in tones of pride and affirmation. Tell them you love them; tell them they are beautiful; tell them they are special. In other words, tell your Scotties all the affirming words *you* long to hear regularly from significant others in your life, but which are rarely spoken except at funerals!

At our *Great Scots Magazine* office my Scotties and I share a special daily ritual. I have a little ditty of a song I made up which celebrates the time for Charlotte to come home in the evening. It goes, *"Is it time? Is it time? Is it time for your Mom to come home?"* Because it is part of our routine, Gus and Willie know when it is "time" by their own internal clocks, and I have merely to sing the first three words to send them into spasms of barking punctuated by vigorous spins and twirls.

Such carryings-on are silly nonsense only to those who do not speak my dog's language. It makes perfect sense to us. That is because all communication is user-specific so that what is most effective is defined by the unique features 'between' the parties communicating. Silly as our little singing ritual may be to anyone not knowing our language, it is effective and memorable communication to us. The point is, when it comes to effective communication between persons or person and dogs one size does not fit all: what works well with one, a tone, a look, a style, does not work as well with another. Individuals are unique and therefore the chemistry between any pair is never the same as between any others. Talk is not the same, either.

Talking to Scotties is no different. In my own experience one responds to a pattern of communication and another does not! My Nati loved to play peek-a-boo and hide-and-seek games. I had merely to get my face near the floor, hiding my eyes behind my hands, or peeking at her around furniture or a corner, to initiate a roaring tussle of mutual delight. But if I peek around a corner at Willie, he barks with alarm and aggression. My point is, optimal communication with your Scottie is a process of your learning to speak their unique 'language' fluently, and then speaking of bonding *in their terms* frequently and affirmingly.

A-H-r-o-o-o-o

Another important aspect of Scottie communication to keep in mind is that Scotties are canids, not mini-people in fur coats. Specifically this means that non-verbal communication, or body-language, is the essence of canine dialogue. All of the para-language features of human talk become critical here: tone, pitch, and rate. So true is this for your doggie communication that you will find *how* you speak to your dogs will affect them more than what you say.

In this all important matter of body language be observant of your Scottie's body language as well as your own. Learn from it and utilize your discoveries to build your own individuated vocabulary of companionship. Recognize the crucial importance of touch as the essential language of bonding. To your Scottie your fingers and hands can say, "I love you," more convincingly than your lips. I find a light circular motion that massages the skin is most effective with my dogs. Nati, our first Scottie, prefered a circular massage on her stomach. Gus prefers his circular massage on his head, neck, and chest. Willie prefers only the back of his neck and his back to be rubbed. My point is, customized touching that affirms by physically connecting a bonded pair is the best investment you can make toward nurturing and deepening your companionship with your dog.

Conclusion

Companionship which is deep and real and lasting, which knits two spirits and nurtures their souls, is rare in our culture of glitz and hype. In these times of throw-away relationships to experience such companionship is to be blessed beyond measure.

Our task as Scottie people is to go beyond seeking great Scottie companions. We must seek to *be* great companions. And we can have no better role model in this arena than to mirror the uncompromising love, loyalty, and devotion our Scotties give to us.

So celebrate your Scotties! Celebrate your companionship! And know that by nurturing the ties that bind, the best is yet to be.

Further Reading

"Scottie Crazies & the Ties That Bind," by Joseph Harvill, is an expanded version of an article first published in ***Great Scots Magazine***, Vol 1 No 1, Jan/Feb 1996.

On the concept of 'betweenness' in interpersonal relationships, see John Stewart, ed. ***Bridges Not Walls: A Book About Interpersonal Communication.*** NY: McGraw-Hill (many editions).

On dog 'talk' and the larger topic of inter-species communication, a light-hearted, but insightful little book is Ronnie Sellers', ***The Official Dog Codependents Handbook: For People Who Love Their Dogs Too Much.*** Kennebunk, ME: Ronnie Sellers Productions, 1996. A deeply serious and profound book is Vicki Hearne, ***Adam's Task: Calling Animals By Name.*** NY: Vintage Books, 1982.

CHAPTER FIVE

Scottie Wisdom For The New Millennium

You may not know it, but you have a little dog to thank for the continuation of time. According to the Shawnee Indian story of creation the world and everything in it was created by Our Grandmother, accompanied by her grandson and her little dog. Daily since the creation She has been weaving a great basket into which she will gather all the souls of the good at the end of time. When the basket is finished the world and all the wicked will end. But every night Her little dog unravels all she has done in one day, so Our Grandmother has slow work getting ahead. Thus the little dog nightly postpones the end of the world.

Mankind, too, has had hard work getting ahead. The last time a new millennium dawned the Normans were on the verge of rule in Britain, Greenland had just been discovered, Europe was coming apart under the Holy Roman Empire, China was facing invading Mongols, India's barbarian Rajputs were threatening the old Hindu Princes, and in the New World, the Old Mayan Empire had disintegrated causing mass migration north to Yucatan.

Difficult as our journey through time has been, it has been friendlier because of man's best friend. As a new millennium dawns for us, it seems appropriate to look to our own little dogs to discover quiet ways by which they, too, keep our personal worlds going during changing times ahead.

I believe the new millennium calls for new ways of thinking about our Scotties, new metaphors by which to better grasp and assimilate the vital re-

Digital art by Joseph Harvill ©2000 Tartan Scottie.

sources our dogs represent in our lives. Let me tease out a few of these new ways to think about our Scotties which can point the way to greater health, happiness, and wisdom in the years ahead.

Scotties As Art

The first new metaphor for our dogs which we need to cultivate for the new millennium is Scotties as fine art.

I was first introduced to this idea of purebred dogs as forms of art in the writings of Roger Caras, the voice of the Westminster Dog Show, who argues convincingly that selective canine breeding at its best is an ancient quest for the ideals of canine form and beauty, and that such a quest by definition is a form of art. To own a pure-bred Scottie today, in other words, is to own a form of masterpiece embodying generations of genetic refinement and persistant quest for the ideal of 'Scottieness.' I believe Caras is right and that purebred dog breeding and ownership in the new millennium is as legitimate as any love of art.

However, the deeper truth about Scotties as art which I wish to emphasize is that, like all art, Scotties are non-utilitarian extravagance. What we need to see is that this is not their weakness; it is their strength for us in the new millennium. Let me explain.

Seeing our dogs as fine art is important because contemporary efficiency and utilitarian thinking threaten our soul by bottom-line definitions of life. Economic models of reality reduce us to what is quantifiable leaving aside values such as beauty, art, and love, and rejecting as inefficient and superfluous cost-intensive Scotties. Our dogs don't make sense in terms of straight line cost-analysis just like preserving large tracts of green space seems a negative economic decision to today's developers. Truth is, our Scotties *are* excessive, both in terms of the demands their care puts upon us, and the attention we readily lavish on them.

From an original painting by Mabel Gear.

My point is that excess is the nature of art. All art is extravagance because the essence of art is passion, and the nature of passion is excess. To economize passion is to destroy it. Love is outrageously generous, abhoring minimums and forever seeking new ways to give. Our problem is our world is shaped by accountants whose focus is the bottom line not love.

That is why our Scotties as fine art mean so much to our future. Few of us grasp art's vital role as art connoisseurs, but we know and love our Scotties. Recognizing our dogs as art can keep us grounded in the vital truth that passion is the soul of the good life and man cannot live by bread alone. The little dogs at our sides can keep us in touch with non-economic values that make life worth living.

Scotties As Fragile

It will appear strange to Scottie lovers to cast the 'Diehard' as fragile. After all, they are tough and fierce to a fault when challenged. Nevertheless, the metaphor of Scotties as fragile is appropriate for the new millennium for important reasons.

One reason has to do with what Classics scholar, Martha Nussbaum, calls "the fragility of goodness." Our beloved Scotties' short lifespans teach us how fragile goodness is. All life hangs by a thread and in a heartbeat it is cut off.

I know it is not pleasant dwelling in the presence of death, nevertheless that is where all life dwells. It is illusions of longevity and fantasies of invulnerability that are unreal. I am often asked, "How long do Scotties live?," and I usually repeat the STCA's 1995 national health survey average— 11.2 years. But, of course, that answer is profoundly misleading, for it implies that somehow Scotties come with a warrantee for 11.2 years!

The truthful answer to the question how long do Scotties live is one day, one breath at a time—just like Scottie owners. And if we knew that today was our last day with our dog how differently we would view our time together! We would savor the moments for all time.

The point is the fragility of goodness is too shear to support taking for granted those we love. Living in the presence of death by seeing our Scotties as fragile is not morbid; it is a wake up call to live and love in the reality of each day.

But Scotties are fragile in another sense, too. Our breed is fragile genetically. Every time Scotties are bred the gene pool is affected. As I write this at the beginning of the 21st century our dogs are 18 times more likely to have bladder cancer than other breeds, yet Scotties remain without a national health registry to enable genetic research to track gene-linked diseases in our breed. National clubs sponsoring Westies and Cairns have established national health registries, but not Scotties, despite our being one of the oldest breeds in the AKC. While gatekeepers ponder, opportunity is lost. How unspeakably sad.

As we move into the new millennium the fragility of goodness must be deeply etched into our consciousness. Our health and vitality hang by the slenderest of threads, and that includes our Scotties. Life is too short and too fragile to take anything for granted.

Scotties As Inner Space

The new millennium dawns for us with a new NASA research project to Mars. Space exploration will feature prominently in the years ahead.

But there is another 'space' sadly neglected, and that is the inner space of the human heart. It is easier and more glamorous to go to Mars, it seems, than it is to go inside ourselves to discover why after so many millennia hate, violence, and war continue to define the human predicament.

Scotties, by contrast, and the magical domain we call companionship, are oases of sanity for us in a world of madness. In contrast to nightly news of drive-by shootings, road-rage, and the decline of civility, the inner space we share with our Scotties surrounds us with unconditional love.

The mini-world we share with our dogs reminds us that inner space is the most important space in our lives. Here is where we nurture relationships. Here is where we nurture our souls.

Scotties as inner space in the new millennium can call us back again and again to the most important space of all— the space between us and those we love.

Scotties As Stories

The fourth metaphor for our Scotties appropriate for the new millennium is Scotties as stories.

Man is Storyteller. From earliest cave walls to the most recent bestselling novel, motion picture or TV sit-com, telling stories is how we make sense of our world and define ourselves.

Scotties bring out the storyteller in us. I have often said, poke a Scottie lover anywhere and out pours a Scottie story! We all do it, quite instinctively. What possesses a modern educated man to draw Scottie petroglyphs on his garden wall?, or eager cyberphiles to proliferate webpages heralding their Scotties?

The answer is: the same thing which led ancient men to tell their stories on cave walls; it is the passion to make permanent the celebrations of the heart!

And dog stories, if they are true to their subject, cannot be anything but extravagant because they tell about not only the dog involved but also about the emotional tone, the heart-zone, which that dog and the storyteller have between them. Our stories are larger than life because our relational bonds with our Scotties are larger than life.

The pragmatic truth here is that life and love are most alive in the telling. Because as humans we construct reality with words, it is in the telling and re-telling of our stories that the psyche forms significance out of the ordinary. It is as if the soul begs for the same stories so it knows something will last. Pity the dog without a story because that dog and that dog owner are without love.

Seeing our Scotties as stories in the new age is invitation to revel in the art of storytelling, invitation to nurture what is primal in our human nature: the passion to magnify celebrations of our hearts.

Scotties As Home

Home is a troubled concept as we drop the curtain on the 20th century. More and more houses spring up everywhere. They're larger and more luxurious than ever, with smaller family units inside. Adjectives of choice these days include "executive-style," "open," and "roomy," but seldom "sweet." Home sweet home has almost disappeared from vocabularies as we enter the 21st century.

Yet it is sweetness which the heart craves because home is fundamentally an emotional state, a place where Thomas Moore says "feelings of security, belonging, placement, family, protection, memory, and personal history abide."

It is no wonder our notions of home, and our quest to find the perfect one, are troubled. Home is a habit of the heart, and when our heart is restless it no longer knows its place.

Trouble is our current rootlessness will likely get worse in the new millennium. As the 20th century uprooted us to distant cities when local companies went national and international, the future will send new generations to frontiers in space.

That is where our Scotties can teach us deep wisdom about heart and home. My dogs are perfectly content wherever they are so long as I am there. Far from home, in strange places, it does not matter. Their center is mobile because it has to do with bonds to a soul-mate, not geography.

Digital art by Tartan Scottie from an original print by Kate Maynard.

Home as soul does not mean in the future we will outgrow homesickness. What it teaches is that if we are wise we will understand what it is about home that fills us with longing, and by knowing what home means we will not seek it in the wrong places.

Seeing our Scotties as home can teach us that home has to do with relationships, not real estate, and that in the 21st century cultivating soul-mates will be more vital to us than monitoring loan rates.

Scotties As Theology

The last of the new metaphors for our Scotties which I see as opportunities for the new millennium is Scotties as theology.

Theology, of course, is talk about God, and that has become problematic for many at the dawn of the 21st century. Oh, there is no shortage of cries from the far right to solve every problem with "more Jesus and more guns," and plenty of televangelism looking just like another Las Vegas celebrity show. But the biblical "still, small voice" of deity is hard to hear in the din of religion as entertainment.

I have spent my life chasing that "still, small voice," or being chased by it! And now in my 50s, in the glitz of religion as spectacle, that voice seems fainter than ever.

I hear it these days— when I hear it at all— not in conventional god-talk but through my Scotties. Jewish philosopher, Martin Buber, once said, "The eyes of an animal have the capacity of a great language." The language I hear from the little dogs at my side is truth about ultimate things; truth about the heart of God.

Digital art by Rebecca and Dan Collins at ArtPaw© @ www.artpaw.com

My Scotties are teaching me to reinterpret contemporary notions of efficiency which drive us to expel whatever has no use, the economic model of life which reduces everything to profit. My Scotties are teaching me generosity through their theology of excess.

I spoke earlier of the danger of comtemporary utilitarian approaches to life which distort values such as art, beauty, and love. Cost-analysis kills generosity because it cannot abide the superfluous.

Yet creation is alive with superfluity and excess. Why *so many* stars? Why *so many* species? Why *such* excess? It is as if God wished to show us he countenances even what seems accidental, trivial, and frivolous, and reveals himself in the excessive and extravagant. God is not manifested in bean-counting but in generosity.

That is where the little dogs at my side speak to me of the divine. Our relationship is excess, pure and simple. Ours is a daily experiment in love and grace where economic models are irrelevant. My Scotties are not bean-counters, and I do not ration my love and care for them. Love, you see, is the opposite of cost-analysis; love mocks minimums.

The Creator mocks minimums and the tyranny of profit, too.

Perhaps the little dogs at our side are messengers to tell us something about grace, about the power of God to love in spite of utility, to create in spite of efficiency, and to give in spite of cost. Perhaps in an age that no longer listens to the voice of God such encounter with our dogs is our "still, small voice" calling us to witness reverence and a plea for love and understanding in the eyes of the useless other. Perhaps in the new millennium to pet a Scottie will not be a bad way to practice theology.

Conclusion

None of us knows what lies ahead. Future shock is now midwife to our culture. Who could have known at the turn of the 20th century we would jump from the birth of aviation to manned spaceflight in little more than fifty years? Like the story of our Grandmother toiling to get ahead in Her weaving we struggle just to keep up with the demands of each new day. And the next 1000 years? Who can say.

Our predicament is a lot like the airline pilot who announced to his passengers that the navigation system was broken and he was unsure where they were heading— but that they should relax because they were making good time! Trouble is, as we rocket into the new millennium what we need most is not speed but *spirit*. In my bones I feel the little dog at our side is an important guide for the days ahead.

Learning to see our Scotties as art, as fragile, as inner space, as stories, as home, and as theology can keep us grounded in values of the heart too easily lost in the rush of progress. The ancient Shawnee Indian story of the cosmic little dog who keeps the world going may turn out to be more important to our health, happiness, and wisdom than we imagine. For in their quiet ways, if we will let them, our dogs can save us from ourselves by unravelling the lethal *busy*ness that chokes our days. Perhaps in the new millennium we, too, will have a little dog to thank for our tomorrow.

Further Reading

Scottie Wisdom For The New Millennium, by Joseph Harvill, first appeared as *Wisdom for the New Millennium: New Ways to Think About Scotties to Keep You Healthy, Happy, & Wise,* in **Great Scots Magazine,** Vol 5 No 1 (Jan/Feb) 2000.

On the concept of the 'fragility of goodness,' see Martha C. Nussbaum, ***The Fragility of Goodness: Luck and Ethics in Greek Tragedy and Philosophy.*** Cambridge: Cambridge University Press, 1986.

Two important books on dogs and theology which I have found stimulating and provocative: Stephen H. Webb, ***On God and Dogs: A Christian Theology of Compassion for Animals.*** Oxford: Oxford University Press, 1998; and Paul Shepard, ***The Others: How Animals Made Us Human.*** Washington, D.C.: Shearwater Books, 1996. For a serious psychological perspective see Eleanora M. Woloy, ***The Symbol of the Dog in the Human Psyche: A Study of the Human-Dog Bond.*** Wilmette, IL: Chiron Publications, 1990.

Part Two:
Nurturing the Scottie Good Life

"Dogs love their friends and bite their enemies, quite unlike people, who are incapable of pure love and always have to mix love and hate in their object relations."

Sigmund Freud

CHAPTER SIX

Test Your Scottie Quotient

Testing human 'Scottie Quotient' is long overdue. Truth is, not everyone is suited to be owned by a Scottie; not every home in the land qualifies as this Highland chieftan's ideal turf. Too often the cute Scottie puppy bought on impulse turns out to be the year-old male terrier abandoned in exasperation at the local humane shelter.

Bad dogs? No. The problem is humans lacking adequate temperament match, or what I call 'Scottie Quotient.'

So far in considering the Scottie good life we have focused on the dog, considering its origins, character, and definitive temperament features, in an effort to better understand the breed. Now it is time to see if you are suited for the dog Scottie lovers call "Mother Nature's class act." Until recently there was no test available by which to pre-test one's Scottie-Quotient, merely hunches and gut-feelings as Scottie veterans tried to advise would-be owners. However, Stanley Coren, Ph.D., professor of psychology at the University of British Columbia, has changed that. His new research, published in his book, ***Why We Love the Dogs We Do*** (1998), offers a simple personality test for matching humans with canine breeds, including the Scottish Terrier.

Coren's Research

Dr. Coren's theory is the age-old match-maker's belief that similarities attract, and that in general, similar traits make better mates. What is new here is his notion of categorizing dogs as well as humans in terms of personality/

temperament profiles, and providing an external test for matching people-types with dog-types.

In collaboration with selected veterinarians, dog obedience trainers, show dog judges, dog behavior analysts, and writers of dog books, Coren first set about to re-categorize the AKC's familiar groupings of dogs along lines of behavioral characteristics instead of function. Coren was seeking temperament traits in the various breeds likely to impact owner compatibility and satisfaction. The outcome is a rough grouping of some 133 popular breeds into seven new categories based on behavioral features which computer analysis indicated were predominant within the new groups.

Digital art ©1999 Tartan Scottie.

Coren's new canine groups based on doggie behavioral tendencies include: **Group 1 Friendly Dogs**, **Group 2 Protective Dogs**, **Group 3 Independent Dogs**, **Group 4 Self-Assured Dogs** (e.g., Scottish Terrier), **Group 5 Consistent Dogs**, **Group 6 Steady Dogs**, and **Group 7 Clever Dogs**. (Sample breeds included in Coren's groupings listed on page 55).

While these new groupings may seem arbitrary at first glance and even pejorative (for example, the categories 'friendly,' and 'clever' hardly convey neutral valence, and imply that breeds not included are 'unfriendly' or 'slow-witted') they are no more so than the traditional groupings of the AKC, which even includes *non*-category classifications (?), e.g., *non-sporting* group, containing Dalmatians and Schipperkes, each of which has proper *working dog* origins! Coren's classification has the merit, from the companion owner's viewpoint, of attempting to address breed behavioral characteristics. If Coren's categories are valid, and if the computer factor-analysis is correct in clustering his perceived dog-traits together, then it would be reasonable to predict that if you like one dog breed in a group, you would probably be compatible with the the others in that group as well.

Beyond re-thinking canine groupings along behavioral lines, Dr. Coren next created a simplified human personality inventory scale. In his judgment, the key predictor of human-canine compatibility is an index of interpersonal traits, not the more typical measures of personality or aptitude. Using as a base the Interpersonal Adjective Scales (IAS) developed by Jerry S. Wiggins, Coren reduced the eight dimensions of the IAS to four, which he named *extroversion*, *dominance*, *trust*, and *warmth*.

Dr. Coren then tested his personality trait and dog group fit by sampling nearly 6,200 people, aged 16 to 94 years. In addition to taking his personality inventory test, each respondent was asked to indicate the breeds of dog they had lived with and their satisfaction with those breeds.

Statistical correlations were then run to determine if, indeed, his human-canine compatibility predictions were statistically valid. The results were positive and impressive. His project was published for scholars in *Journal of Research in Personality* (1994) and further refined for his book, ***Why We Love the Dogs We Do*** (1998). In Dr. Coren's ground-breaking work we now have a first of its kind tool for human-canine match-making.

Implications

Dr. Coren's research, and particularly his underlying assumptions, are, of course, open to debate. For example, his breed stereotyping leaves untouched the huge question of mixed-breed dogs, and his assumptions regarding breed behavior ignore the debate over nature vs. nurture, apparently assuming that canine behavior is all 'hard-wired.'

Still, kibitzing aside, his work is a giant step toward taking the guesswork out of dog breed selection.

Among the potential benefactors of Dr. Coren's research are canine rescue organizations. The crucial part of Scottie Rescue, for example, is effective screening of applicants in order to prevent recurrent abandonment. Dr. Coren's personality test offers a simple and objective index for assessing compatibility with our breed.

Breeders could help our breed, too, by utilizing Coren's test when placing puppies. While his test is not necessarily the last word in assessing whether a new owner is 'right' for our breed, it could be an important first indicator of incompatibilities.

The implications are exciting for Scottie lovers: whether it's a new puppy buyer or a re-homing prospect, the time to discover mismatches is before they happen. Dr. Stanley Coren's new research puts in our hands a simple diagnostic tool which can help us measure the critical predictor of bonding with the breed we love— 'Scottie Quotient.'

The Test

It is time to ask and answer the question, is this the right dog for your version of the good life? Or put another way, it is time to turn the tables to see if *you* fit the personality profile preferred by the Scottish Terrier. Are you suitable to be owned by a Scottie?

Here is a simple test which can help you answer that question, and perhaps help avoid mismatches. It provides your own personal scores on four personality traits which are keys for canine breed choice and dog ownership.

The test consists of a set of words which describe personal characteristics, along with the definitions of those words. For each word you must decide how accurately the term 'fits' YOU. Your answer is chosen from an 8-point rating scale, ranging from "extremely inaccurate" to "extremely accurate." For example, if you feel the test word/question is an *extremely accurate* description of you, then you would write the number 8 on the line to the left of the question, but if you feel the test word only *slightly accurately* describes your general behavior, then you would write the number 5 on the line, etc.

Do not spend too long pondering each individual word. Generally, your first impressions of your personality are the most accurate. Beware, too, the natural tendency to want to appear perfect. This is not about 'Ms. Nice Person,' but about compatibilities, so there are no bad answers or answerers. Be as truthful as you can, and forget about what is or is not flattering since to your canine companion flattery does not count, anyway.

Rating Scale

1. Extremely inaccurate
2. Very inaccurate
3. Moderately inaccurate
4. Slightly inaccurate
5. Slightly accurate
6. Moderately accurate
7. Very accurate
8. Extremely accurate

HOW ACCURATELY DO THESE WORDS DESCRIBE YOU? FILL IN THE NUMBER FROM THE RATING SCALE ABOVE THAT CORRESPONDS TO YOUR ANSWER.

_____ **Shy:** you lack self-confidence and tend to be uncomfortable around other people.

_____ **Undemanding:** you do not demand or expect much from other people.

_____ **Gentle-hearted:** you are warm or kind to other people.

_____ **Outgoing:** you enjoy meeting other people.

_____ **Assertive:** you tend to be aggressive and outspoken with other people.

_____ **Cunning:** you are crafty, skillful at manipulating others, and a bit devious.

____ **Unsympathetic:** you are not easily swayed or emotionally moved by people's problems.

____ **Introverted:** you feel more comfortable by yourself and less interested in having people around.

____ **Unaggressive:** you tend to be mild-mannered and not forceful around others.

____ **Not Deceptive:** you are not tricky or misleading, and tend to be straightforward when dealing with others.

____ **Kind:** you are thoughtful, caring, and accomodating to other people.

____ **Friendly:** you like to be with others and you are open and warm around them.

____ **Dominant:** you tend to lead others and like to command and take charge in a group.

____ **Tricky:** you can be deceiving, or able to fool others, to get what you want.

____ **Hard-Hearted:** you are unconcerned about other people and don't care much about their feelings.

____ **Unsociable:** you do not enjoy meeting people or being in the company of others.

Scottie Quotient Rating Score Card
Measuring Extroversion, Dominance, Trust, Warmth

Proceed to the 'Rating Score Card' (right and next pages) where you will transfer to the score card blanks the numbers entered for the previous word-association test questions (on the previous page and above). Use the final calculations on each score card to score your personality traits of Extroversion, Dominance, Trust, and Warmth.

EXTROVERSION

1. Add the following two scores and then add 20.

   ____ **Friendly**
   + ____ **Outgoing**
   + 20
   = ____ Total 1

2. Add the following two scores.

   ____ **Introverted**
   + ____ **Unsociable**
   = ____ Total 2

3. Next subtract Total 2 from Total 1.

   ____ Total 1
   − ____ Total 2
   = ____ Your **Extroversion** Score

*Check which applies

   ___ High
   ___ Medium
   ___ Low

   *Women: 28 or above = High; 20 or below = Low; 21-27 = Medium
   *Men: 28 or above = High; 19 or less = Low; 20-27 = Medium

TRUST

1. Add the following two scores and then add 20.

   ___ **Undemanding**

   + ___ **Not Deceptive**

   + 20

   = ___ Total 1

2. Add the following two scores.

   ___ **Cunning**

   + ___ **Tricky**

   = ___ Total 2

3. Next subtract Total 2 from Total 1.

   ___ Total 1

   − ___ Total 2

   = ___ Your **Trust** Score

*Check which applies

___ High
___ Medium
___ Low

*Women: 26 or above = High; 18 or below = Low;
19-25 = Medium
*Men: 25 or above = High; 18 or less = Low
19-24 = Medium

DOMINANCE

1. Add the following two scores and then add 20.

   ___ **Dominant**

   + ___ **Assertive**

   + 20

   = ___ Total 1

2. Add the following two scores.

   ___ **Shy**

   + ___ **Unaggressive**

   = ___ Total 2

3. Next subtract Total 2 from Total 1.

   ___ Total 1

   − ___ Total 2

   = ___ Your **Dominance** Score

*Check which applies

___ High
___ Medium
___ Low

*Women: 23 or above = High; 16 or below = Low;
17-22 = Medium
*Men: 24 or above = High; 18 or less = Low
19-23 = Medium

WARMTH

1. Add the following two scores and then add 20.

    ___ Kind
  + ___ Gentle-Hearted
  + 20
  = ___ Total 1

2. Add the following two scores.

    ___ Hard-Hearted
  + ___ Unsympathetic
  = ___ Total 2

3. Next subtract total 2 from Total 1.

    ___ Total 1
  − ___ Total 2
  = ___ Your **Warmth** Score

*Check which applies

___ High
___ Medium
___ Low

*Women: 30 or above = High; 23 or below = Low; 24-29 = Medium
*Men: 28 or above = High; 20 or less = Low; 21-28 = Medium

*For interpretation of scores and the personality types most suited for Scotties, see below.

Scottie Quotient Test Match-Up

In general, Dr. Coren suggests that a breed match on any two or more of the four personality trait dimensions indicates strong 'match' compatibility with dogs of that group.

People Scotties Prefer to Own

Women	Low Extroversion High Dominance Low Trust Low Warmth
Men	Medium Extroversion High Dominance Low Trust [warmth measures did not show up on Dr. Coren's factor analysis]

Personality All-Breed Match-Up

Table 1
Dog groups that are most preferred by men and women with differing levels of extroversion

Extroversion Score	Dog Groups For Women	Men
High	Independent Protective	Consistent Clever
Medium	Consistent Clever	Friendly Self-Assured
Low	Steady Self-Assured	Independent Steady

Table 2
Dog groups that are most preferred by men and women with differing levels of dominance

Dominance Score	Dog Groups For Women	Men
High	Self-Assured Steady	Self-Assured Steady
Medium	Consistent Friendly	Friendly Clever
Low	Protective Independent	Protective Independent

Table 3
Dog groups that are most preferred by men and women with differing levels of trust

Trust Score	Dog Groups For Women	Men
High	Consistent Protective	Protective Clever
Medium	Friendly Consistent	Friendly Independent
Low	Steady Self-Assured	Steady Self-assured

Table 4
Dog groups that are most preferred by men and women with differing levels of warmth

Warmth Score	Dog Groups For Women	Men
High	Protective Friendly	Clever Friendly
Medium	Independent Clever	Protective Independent
Low	Self-Assured Steady	Steady Consistent

*See Dr. Coren's book for full taxonomy of breeds into his seven groups, *Friendly, Protective, Independent, Self-Assured* (the Scottie group), *Consistent, Steady,* and *Clever* dogs. Some categories appear more pejorative than descriptive (e.g., 'friendly' and 'clever'), nevertheless Coren's seven groups represent a fresh attempt to classify canines according to temperament types. Examples of the dogs included in the seven groups follow:

Group 1: Friendly Dogs— e.g., Bichon Frise, Border Terrier, Cocker Spaniel, Collie, Golden Retriever, Labrador Retriever.

Group 2: Protective Dogs— e.g., Akita, Boxer, Bullmastiff, Chow, Rottweiler, Schnauzers (standard & giant), Weimaraner.

Group 3: Independent Dogs— e.g., Afghan Hound, Airedale, Dalmatian, Shar-Pei, Greyhound, Irish Setter.

Group 4: Self-Assured Dogs— e.g., Australian Terrier, Basenji, Cairn, Fox Terrier, Jack Russell, Schnauzer (miniature), Scottie, Westie.

Group 5: Consistent Dogs— e.g., Boston Terrier, Dachshund, Lhasa Apso, Pomeranian, Pug, Sealyham Terrier, Whippet.

Group 6: Steady Dogs— e.g., Basset Hound, Beagle, Bulldog, Great Dane, Saint Bernard.

Group 7: Clever Dogs— e.g., Border Collie, Corgi, Doberman Pinscher, German Shepherd, Poodle.

Further Reading

"Test Your Scottie Quotient," by Joseph Harvill, is an expanded revision of an earlier article, *"How High is Your S.Q.?—Measuring Your Scottie Quotient for 'That Scottie in the Window,'"* first published in *Great Scots Magazine*, Vol 3 No 6, Nov/Dec 1998.

Stanley Coren, *Why We Love the Dogs We Do: How To Find the Dog That Matches Your Personality.* N.Y.: The Free Press, 1998.

On technical matters relating to Dr. Coren's personality test and its reliability see: Stanley Coren, *Journal of Research in Personality* 28 (1994): 214-29; J.S. Wiggins and R. Broughton, *European Journal of Personality* 5 (1991): 342-65; J.S. Wiggins, *Journal of Personality Assessment* 66 (1996): 217-33.

For an alternative approach to breed selection and a test to see which is right for you, see the Purina website at *www.purina.com*. They offer a helpful breed selector 'test' which is aimed at pet owners who wish to make informed choices. Thanks to Colleen Schiller for this suggestion.

CHAPTER SEVEN

Well-Begun Is Half-Done: Finding The Right Scottie Puppy

Carole Fry Owen

My phone rings several times a week with someone pleading, "Can you help me find a Scottie?" Sometimes the caller is in tears because he's just lost an old Scottie that was part of the heart, and I want so much to pull a Scottie out of my magic bag. Since shopping for a Scottie in the right places is not like going to the mall, callers usually find Mother Owen's cupboard bare of Scotties, but I and many other breeders enjoy starting callers on a successful search.

If no Scottie stories pour forth from the receiver, my first question is: "Have you owned Scotties before?" There are many reasons these innocents might not like a Scottie, and I tell them that! Some of those reasons are the very reasons you and I would not own any other breed. No pushbutton Poodles or Golden Retrievers for us! We like challenges and spice.

Scotties are an acquired taste. They are not the dog for many families. Why should we offer a glass of Glenfiddich to someone who prefers Koolaid? Un-Scottied callers need help. I tell them how to obtain important information to help them decide if the Scottish Terrier is the right breed for them.

Here is how a typical search might begin when you, a true Scottiephile, call a serious breeder. Take my own routine as an example.

First, I will ask if you have the Scottish Terrier Club of America's Information Packet. Anyone trying to locate a Scottie, even persons who already

Check-list Test Questions for Rating Breeders

(1) Are you a member of a Scottie club?
Quality breeders join Scottie clubs to learn more about the breed and to establish friendships with owners working for the welfare of Scotties.

(2) Do you sell other breeds besides Scotties?
Ideal breeders breed only Scotties. Breeders of multiple breeds are usually commercial producers who are less knowledgable about Scotties.

(3) What problems can I expect from Scotties?
If the breeder does not point out undesirable characteristics, you know you're talking to someone eager (or desperate) to sell dogs to the first comer.

(4) Do you offer a trial period?
Many responsible breeders do and also offer to take the Scottie back at any time in its life. Responsible breeders want the buyer to have the 'right' Scottie, and will stand by that Scottie for a lifetime.

(5) Do you require spay or neuter?
Many responsible breeders require their puppies be spayed and neutered. Some offer refunds upon proof of spay/neuter. These breeders want to prevent descendants of their puppies from misuse by puppymills or backyard breeders. They also realize that spaying and neutering reduces the risk of various cancers.

(6) Do you own both parents?
Veteran breeders sometimes own both parents, but more usually do not. Rather, they choose a male with qualities to complement their female, even if that male lives 1,000 miles away.

---

know the breed, should have this material. (To obtain the Scottie information packet, send $2 to Joanne Kinnelly, STCA Public Information Chairman, 3684 N. Prospect Rd., Ann Arbor, MI 48105).

Usually I will know several breeders with Scotties available for sale and will suggest you contact them. The secret to finding a Scottie is: CALL, and keep calling. If one breeder does not have a dog that meets your needs, ask her to suggest other breeders. She will, and it is in your best interests to talk with many breeders. You will learn something from each one. Eventually you will decide, "I've got to have a Scottie from this person. I like how he talks about Scotties."

Next, I tell you how to reach the two or three regional Scottie clubs nearest your home. Club secretaries are knowledgeable about which members have puppies, adults or rescues available. You will end up with more prospects, and each of them can give you still more referrals. Once you are "in the

(7) Do your Scotties have skin problems?

If the breeder answers "no," ask him what he knows about the parents, grandparents and siblings of his breeding stock. Most casual breeders know nothing about the health of their dogs' relatives. Skin problems are hereditary and will be a 10-15-year pain and expense for you and your Scottie.

(8) Have the sire and dam been DNA-tested "clear" of the VWD gene?

If the answer is "yes" for either parent, you guarantee your Scottie will not have vonWillebrand's Disease, a devastating bleeding disorder. Most commercial breeders are unaware of the VWD DNA test, or do not want to spend the money.

(9) What can you tell me about Scottie Cramp, Cranial Mandibular Osteopathy and von Willebrand's Disease?

If a breeder cannot tell you lots about these diseases, they will know nothing about other Scottie health problems. You are playing Russian roulette if you buy from this kind of breeder.

(10) May I see your sales agreement?

Responsible breeders use sales agreements in which they outline their own responsibilities to the buyer, and what they require of the buyer (terms like spay/neuter and the right of "first refusal" if the buyer later does not want the dog). A simple bill of sale is not a sales agreement.

---

loop" and sell yourself as the ideal Scottie owner, a successful search is guaranteed, assuming you are patient. You will not get in the loop when you call a classified ad offering Scotties for sale. That is a deadend.

There are 20 regional Scottie clubs affiliated with the American Kennel Club. Though the clubs may be miles from you, their members come from a still larger area. Breeders who belong to a regional club, an all-breed dog club, and/or the Scottish Terrier Club of America must sign codes of ethics. Buying from a club member is insurance that the breeder is interested in more than your dollars. Do not rule out buying a long distance Scottie, when you find the right breeder.

"But I just want a pet," callers often reply when I point them to a breeder who shows dogs— as if it does not matter where they buy a Scottie. Buying from a show breeder is like buying from someone who has a Ph.D. in Scotties instead of from someone who left high school before finishing the Scottie course. Every show breeder sells puppies and older dogs to premium pet homes. You may even find a wonderful retired champion available for a very reasonable price. Remember, *Great Scots Magazine* readers are the experienced Scottie owners veteran breeders prefer.

The enchanting character of the Scottie pup. Photo by Robert Gannon.

Keep an open mind when looking for a Scottie. If you absolutely must have an eight-week-old black female, you make your search very difficult. You have already eliminated any black males, or brindles and wheatens of either sex that may be ready for homes. Specify a color, sex and age, and you sabotage your search. Anyway, color should be the last thing that matters.

Patience pays! When you find a breeder you like who doesn't have a Scottie available, ask if he keeps a waiting list. Many excellent breeders breed no more than one litter a year, and usually keep one or more puppies themselves "to grow out." Choosing a Scottie from such a breeder is to buy from an artisan.

Avoid pet shop Scotties. (I know you know that). An instant Scottie is not your answer, especially when that instant Scottie comes with an unknown health background and is bred by someone who does not care enough about his puppies to choose who buys them. Soft hearts should stay out of pet stores. If we care about our breed, we should not perpetuate commercial breeding of Scotties. Every Scottie bought from a pet shop encourages that retailer to find another to sell. If you buy from a reseller (the pet shop), you will receive no help and advice from the breeder; you will know nothing about the health background of your puppy; you will miss the joy of becoming part of a larger Scottie family and sharing the antics of your Scottie with its breeder throughout its life; and you will pay far more money than the puppy is worth.

Life Lesson #1 which we have all learned is: You usually get what you pay for. That is not the case with pet shop puppies. They are over-priced. However, a responsible breeder who completes genetic testing and health screening on his breeding stock deserves to receive more compensation for his Scotties than a backyard breeder. A breeder who tests his breeding stock in the show ring is able to offer quality pets that are close to the AKC's Scottish Terrier Standard in conformation and temperament. He rightly will charge more than the person who breeds two Scotties just because they have AKC registration numbers.

What will you pay for a Scottie pet? Probably $500 to $800 if you buy from someone who tries to produce quality Scotties. Yes, you can find a Scottie in the newspaper for $250 or $300. Will the money you save be worth it? Does it matter where you buy a Scottie? You decide.

My last suggestions are the most simple: If a breeder seems too eager to sell you a Scottie, do not buy! If a breeder does not ask you many questions about your family and home, do not buy! Buyer beware!

The right Scottie is out there for you. If you are like me when I look for antique Scottie collectibles, the search is half the fun. Look at your search for a real Scottie in the same way.

©1999 Carole Owen

Photo by Doris Wickersham.

*This chapter first appeared as *"Can You Help Me Find a Scottie?"* in *GSM* Vol 4 No 2 (Mar/Apr) 1999, and was nominated for 'Best Article In A Single Breed Magazine' by the Dog Writers Association of America for 1999.

TO LOCATE BREEDERS AND RESCUE PROGRAMS, CONTACT:

1) Susan Clarkson, STCA Corresponding Secretary, 136 Clunie Dr., Sacramento, CA 95864. Phone: 916/ 483-9069. Email: dueanger@pacbell.net.
2) Daphne and Marshall Branzell, STCA Rescue Chairpersons, 5810 Windvale Dr., Windcrest, TX 78239. Phone: 210/ 653-3723; Email: scotswind@aol.com.
3) STCA Internet pages: http://clubs.akc.org/stca/

*Club officers change. Information above is current in 2000. For current officers contact AKC Customer Service, 5580 Centerview Dr., Raleigh, NC. Phone: 919/ 233-9767; FAX 919 233 3627; E-mail> info@akc.org. http://www.akc.org.

CHAPTER EIGHT

Puppy Bootcamp

Ginger McAfee

Let us assume you have done your homework and have decided a Scottie puppy is for you. If you have never been owned by a Scottie I would encourage you to talk with, and even visit people who share their home with one or more adult Scotties. Make absolutely sure this is the breed for you because taking a Scottie into your home is a lifetime commitment and it simply is not the case that every home should have one. Scotties are special and need special homes. However, I have discovered that after having a Scottie most people will not be satisfied with another breed.

Choose The Right Breeder

Now, after choosing the breed, it is on to choosing a breeder. A caring, reputable breeder can be located in several ways, and a step-by-step plan is outlined elsewhere in this book. You are not likely to find one in the local newspaper. Visit dog shows and talk to people there, check the dog magazines, ask people who own Scotties to recommend their breeder, and do not forget to consider Scottie Rescue. Second-hand Scotties make first-rate pets!

Take Personal Inventory

After you have located a breeder with whom you are comfortable, don't be surprised to learn you will have to wait. And do not be offended when the breeder asks you such questions as: "Have you had a Scottie before? How will the puppy be housed and cared for? Is your yard fenced and secure? Will you be absent from the house most of the day? Are there children in the home? Do you plan to breed?" The breeder is not being nosey but rather simply desires to place Scotties only with caring and responsible families. Also by discerning your life-style the breeder may be able to help you choose the perfect puppy.

I suggest you eliminate from your thinking the notion of 'pick of the litter' because each Scottie puppy is unique and special so each one is the 'pick' for a special home suited just for him. You want to choose the puppy that will be your 'pick of the litter.'

The next step in the process is to take serious inventory of your home and lifestyle. If your home is very active you will need an active puppy. If, however, you live a more sedate life, perhaps a quieter pup or even an adult would be best suited for you. With these criteria in mind, make a list of what you would realistically want in a companion, then contact your chosen breeder to see when a litter is due.

On-site Visit

Ideally the next step would be to visit the breeder when the puppies are about eight weeks old to select your puppy. Look for clear eyes and shiny coats. Techniques to aid your selection might include: sitting down and noting which puppy comes first and which one lags behind; which one crawls into your lap; which one pulls at your sleeve. You can crumple up a piece of paper

From an original print by Morgan Dennis. Joseph Harvill Collection.

to see which puppy is interested in the noise, and which is fearful. Bring a squeaky toy and observe individual responses.

Ask to see the parents of the litter and make sure they look healthy (remember: the mother will not look her best just after whelping and nursing a litter of active youngsters!). If there is something you do not like about the parents of the litter then resume your search because puppies tend to follow their genes and take after their dam and sire.

If you like the parents and the litter ask the breeder about differences she has observed in the litter. A caring breeder will not try to sell you a puppy but will want to place each Scottie in the home that suits it best. Good breeders will be eager to share their observations on each puppy.

Questions & Contracts

Ask explicitly about health issues. Ask if there has been any Scottie Cramp, Demodex, Cranial Mandibular Osteopathy (Terrier Jaw), or vonWillebrand's Disease within the bloodlines. If the breeder does not know about these potential problems move on to the next breeder on your list. Responsible breeders will have done their homework and will be eager to answer these health questions. Do not hesitate to ask for references of people who have obtained Scotties from her, and also ask the name of her veterinarian. Similarly, do not be surprised when good breeders ask you for references as well!

Reputable breeders will give you a guarantee in writing as to the health of your puppy, its show quality assessment, and spay or neuter contracts. Also she should be willing to take the Scottie back if you are no longer able to care for it. Do not expect a refund beyond the stated period in the contract, but good breeders will take back one of their dogs and find it a new home. All such guarantees and agreements in writing distinguish breeders who are commited to nurturing the breed from those merely selling puppies.

Unfortunately, the above ideal scenario for selecting your puppy is rarely possible. More often, you choose your breeder, discuss with her the above needs and desires, find out when she has a litter due and ask to be placed on her list to be notified when the puppies come. By giving the breeder clear search criteria, for example, color, gender, temperament, she can more nearly match a Scottie that may be right for you. If you cannot visit the breeder and her Scotties, ask to see pictures and pedigrees of the parent dogs, as well as references of someone with offspring from that breeding pair. Ask for pictures of the litter and of the puppy the breeder is holding for you.

Wise Consumers

Let me add here that if you are looking for a companion Scottie, coat color and gender should be the last items of concern. Scotties come in many lovely colors, and color preference is not a sin. But do not discount a Scottie just by color. Similarly, I have not found a great deal of difference for companionship between genders. As a companion your puppy should be spayed or neutered at about six months of age, anyway, which means your Scottie will never know what sex he or she is, so the gender choice is somewhat moot, anyway.

Bringing Puppy Home

The day you pick up your puppy finally arrives and it is almost like bringing home a new baby. You have made plans and preparations in advance and you are ready to welcome this new arrival into your home.

Your advance planning needs to include exactly where your puppy will spend his first few days in your home. You may want to section off part of your kitchen, utility room or bathroom and line the floor with newspaper. Puppy proof this area, and in fact, all of the house where your puppy will be allowed to roam. Get down on all fours and look for exposed wires, low hanging table coverings, and expensive decorations that may be a temptation to a young pup. Eliminate problems before they begin by removing temptations. You can always return them after your puppy is mature enough to leave things alone. A friend of mine observed that there is a direct correlation between the item on which a puppy wants to chew and the price you paid for it!

From an original print by Morgan Dennis in the editor's collection.

When you go to get your puppy, take along an empty bottle and ask the breeder to supply some of the water the puppy has been accustomed to drinking. Give him this water on the trip home, and once there, mix it with your local water for a few days. If this is not possible, try commercial bottled water. This can help prevent stomach reactions and diarrhea. Also, either get a sample of the puppy's familiar food from the breeder or make certain you can get that brand. If you plan to switch brands, do so gradually, mixing the different foods for a few days and tapering off the discontinued food.

First Night

The first night will be traumatic for your new puppy. He is away from the only family he has known. Experts differ on how you should manage your first night together. Some suggest putting him into his crate with some soft towels and a stuffed toy. Place the crate as far away from your bedroom as possible. Turn off all the lights and confidently say 'good night.' Monitor his crying, but go to him only if his sounds indicate physical distress. If you rescue him at this point he soon learns that crying gets results, and he begins training you rather than the other way around.

Other experts seem to say it is better to have the pup's sleeping crate in the room with you so you can soothe him when he cries. This might be a workable situation, and seems preferable for the pup. If this works for you, I still advise not rescuing him from his crate. It is amazing how quickly a puppy learns to control his people. One lady was still getting up to take her dog outside several times throughout the night after the dog was well over a year old! Once outside, the Scottie wanted to play. He had trained his owner very well! I suggested that the next time he awakened her in the middle of the night she take him to his crate and leave him there the rest of the night. She did this for three consecutive nights and he was cured.

Whatever your choice of sleeping locations, avoid rough and tumble play just before bed time and be sure to allow him time to eliminate after his last feeding. I do not suggest putting water in his sleeping crate unless you are using the type of external water bottle that fastens to the outside of the wire door. A turned-over water dish and wet bed do not promote rest.

Be sure to take him to his 'potty place' outdoors as soon as you awake in the morning. Do not let his feet touch the floor, but scoop him up from the crate and take him straight to the appropriate place outside to eliminate. Your pup will try his best to avoid soiling his sleeping quarters, and your studious attention to facilitating bladder and bowel eliminations last thing at night and first thing in the morning will reinforce his resolve.

Toilet Training

If your puppy is younger than sixteen weeks his muscles have not developed enough to allow him much bladder control. Therefore toilet training will consist of just getting him used to the area where you want him to eliminate. Right now he will move his bowels after each meal and first thing in the morning. He will wet every three or four hours. The first few months you will spend much of your time taking puppy outside, and the rest of the time wishing you had taken him out sooner!

House training is a learning process which requires patience and consistency. Establish a routine from the first day your puppy arrives. Remember that since a young puppy has very little control of bladder and bowels you must anticipate his needs. Harsh discipline at any stage of house-breaking will be detrimental to your goals. I have found crate training is the best method. A size 200 crate (20 inches by 27 inches by 19 inches high) is a good size and will be useable all of your dog's life. His crate should become his den and he should be crated unless you are attending to his needs or are playing with him. Never give a puppy unsupervised run of the house until he can be trusted regarding chewing and soiling.

Take your new puppy to the designated toilet area upon awakening, after each meal, and frequently in between these times. Always take her to this spot every time you take her from her crate. I find it useful to use a word that you want her to associate with elimination. I use 'potty' but you may choose any term you think appropriate. When she eliminates say, "Good potty, GOOD potty!" Praise, praise, praise and use the trigger word often. Sometimes dogs are reluctant to eliminate in a strange place when traveling, so if you have taught her a trigger-word she associates with eliminating you can give her permission to use a different toilet area.

Some people use treats as motivation for housetraining, but this can be problematic. I recently spoke to a woman using this method on her two Scottie puppies. She complained it took her wee wise guys only a couple of weeks to hijack her scheme to their own purposes. They quickly learned if they went outside and came back in, they got a treat. Soon they were going to the door, running into the yard, and racing back for their treat, completely missing the point of the trip outside!

In case of accidents— and there will be accidents— wash the affected area with a solution of soapy water mixed with a little vinegar. Do not use an ammonia based cleaner as it will attract him to the spot.

Some time after six months of age your puppy should be ready to understand what is expected of him and physically be able to comply. If you should witness his making an unwanted deposit, scold him and pick him up, along with the deposit, and take both him and the evidence out to the designated toilet area, place the evidence where he should eliminate, show it to him and praise him, by smiling and saying, "Good potty." Then take them both back into the house, place the deposit back on the floor, frown and say, "Bad boy!" Do this at least twice for each mistake. Remember this is effective only AF-

TER he is mature enough to understand and to physically comply with what is expected of him. It is never acceptable to rub his nose in it, or any other form of harsh discipline. Your Scottie really wants to please you and he will get the hang of it as soon as he can.

If you cannot be with your puppy during the day I suggest you section off a safe area and use newspaper or housebreaking pads. You cannot expect a puppy or an adult dog to stay crated all day or to 'hold it' that long. This practice may even be hard on their kidneys and should never be routine. If you are not going to have time to invest in appropriate housetraining, perhaps you should rethink your decision to get a puppy.

Socialization

Ideally, your puppy has already begun the socialization process with his breeder who has handled and loved him on a daily basis. You may also want to do some simple dominance exercises, the design of which is to establish early and clearly the dog's subordinate role in your family.

Hold the puppy up in front of your face and look him directly in the eyes until he looks away. If he continues to stare at you, he may be challenging your authority. As soon as he looks away, hold him close to you, placing your chin over the back of his neck and praise, praise, praise.

The dominance-down, or 'alpha roll,' is a good way to teach your puppy that you are in charge in his new family. Begin with several times a day, as you are playing with your pup, roll him over and gently pin him on his side. If he struggles, give a deep-throated correction, "No!" that sounds almost like a growl. As soon as he relaxes, praise him and release him.

The socialization training is not to be administered in an abusive manner, but should be a gentle but firm affirmation of who is the leader of your dog's pack and a means to establish early your control over him. Such unambiguous control is neither demeaning nor negative, but promotes harmony and can be important to your Scottie's safety, especially in emergency situations. A dog that ignores its owner's command is a jeopardy to itself and to others. There is no need to be brutal. Your goal is to establish control over your Scottie, and as she learns to submit to your control you can taper off these exercises and discontinue them altogether by six months, when she will be ready for puppy kindergarten classes.

Preventive Health Care

You should schedule a visit to your veterinarian within the first few days of having your puppy home. This will put your mind at ease about your new dog's health and get the schedule to complete his shots. You should take along a fresh stool sample to be tested for parasites. Never allow a young puppy to roam in the waiting room at the veterinarian's office. After all, this is where sick dogs come. Leave the puppy in the car unless it is too hot or cold outside. Go in to register your visit, and fetch the puppy after you have been given a room assignment. If you do take your puppy into the waiting room, hold him on your lap and avoid contact with other dogs until he has had the complete series of vaccinations. Never allow a puppy that has not completed his shots to have access to any area where stray dogs could have been, such as a public park or roadside rest area. If you must travel with him for a great distance take along plenty of newspapers and line the trunk of your car with them and allow your pup to run inside the trunk while you are stopped at a rest area. With luck, he will use this opportunity to urinate and defecate. If not, it is better to clean up a soiled crate than risk your new puppy's health and perhaps even his life.

Obedience

Teaching a puppy to 'sit' and 'stay' are the two most helpful commands he can learn. It is never pleasant to go into a home where a dog is uncontrolable and the owners must grab him every time the door is opened just to keep him from bolting outdoors. These are also safety commands at home. Scotties, generally, cannot be trusted unsupervised in an unfenced area. So you need to teach your dog to sit and stay every time the door is open. This will give you freedom to carry items in and out without fear your Scottie will run out the door.

Begin when he is at least ten weeks old and before 16 weeks. He should be already used to a collar and lead. Put these on him and I suggest getting a treat such as small bits of cheese. Get on his level, hold one hand under his neck and the other on his rear. Push him into a sitting position, all the while giving the command, "sit." Say it several times. Keep your hand under his neck to hold him in the position but use the other hand to stroke him saying, "Good sit, good sit!" several times, then plop a treat in his mouth. Anytime he raises his rear say, "No, SIT." Repeat this up to five times, then rest and you can repeat the process a couple of times a day.

After a few days, just put your hand under his neck but don't push him into the sitting position. Repeat the process and give him a chance to obey the command the next day. Keep this up several times a day, even after he has learned it, then practice several times a week after that.

When you feel your Scottie has mastered the 'sit' command, go on to 'stay.' Put him into the 'sit' position with his collar and lead on. You should be standing and he should be sitting by your left foot. Hold the lead on your left hand and then with your right hand open, palm toward the dog, bring it down to almost touch his nose with your palm and say, "Stay." As soon as he bolts up push him into the sitting position and say, "NO, stay." Do not use many words, just these terse command terms. Maintain eye contact and hold the lead. If he gets up, you have the lead to keep him near.

After he has gotten the idea keep holding the lead and take a step to your right. Continue eye contact. Go back to him and praise him by saying, "GOOD stay! Good stay!" Give him a treat and release him with an "OK."

Repeat this a few times each day. You will soon be able to step away and move to his front to the length of the lead. The next step is to drop the lead and move all the way around him and he should stay in a sit position, maintaining eye contact. Move farther and farther away for greater lengths of time. Then go back to him and praise him and release him with the 'OK' command when the practice session is over.

The rest of his training should come through an obedience class but these simple commands could be taught early and thoroughly even if no formal classes are taken. Every time you go in or out the door, put him on 'sit, stay,' and soon he will get the idea he is not to run out the door just because it opens.

Conditioning

While helping your new puppy become a well-behaved member of your household remember that puppies should always receive acknowledgment for their actions. Good behavior should be rewarded by treats and/or liberal praise. The tone of your voice is more important than what you say. Undesirable behavior should also be corrected immediately. Timing is everything, since dogs associate rewards and correction with the act that is currently taking place. Your Scottie cannot relate to reinforcement of an activity that occurred prior to the reaction, so taking a dog back to a deed done in your absence is never effective. Corrections and praise must be done in-the-act or your Scottie will never understand what you want of him.

In addition to tone of voice, remember that facial expression ought to match your verbal communication. Smile as you praise; scowl when you reprimand.

You should also spend time grooming your puppy. I suggest placing him on a table or stool to brush him as this will not be confused with play time on the floor or in your lap. The height may also lessen his activity as he is learning to be groomed. Rub his feet and toes often, look into his mouth and even brush his teeth. Not only will this give you the chance to observe any changes in feet and mouth, it will get him accustomed to being handled by the vet and the groomer.

Biting

Young Scotties tend to be 'mouthy' and can be over stimulated by excessive petting. Mouthiness is somewhat normal but now is the time to correct and control the behavior. I believe this innate tendency comes from their origins as ratters, bred to rid barn and home of vermin. Young Scotties feel an overwhelming need to chase everything that moves, such as hands and feet. Such biting should not be interpreted as aggression but it should be corrected, by scruff shakes, nose thumps, or squirts from a water bottle. Never swat your puppy with your hand or with newspapers.

A Scottie pup's natural instinct to chase and bite moving targets presents a special problem for children. Young puppies have very sharp teeth and many injuries attributed to a dog bite are in fact merely the puppy behaving in a manner consistent to the breed. Young children should be taught to respect the new Scottie's mouthy tendency, and instructed never to jerk their hands away and never to tease. It is best to monitor child and puppy together until your pup and the child know proper behavior.

Teaching your Scottie bite control is an important part of socialization. Some trainers recommend yelling loudly when puppy bites toes or fingers. The shout startles him and he will learn that his biting hurts you. Litter mates cry out when play gets too rough, and your puppy's mother corrected him with a scruff shake and a growl whenever he bit too hard on her. Such maternal discipline can be imitated by grabbing the loose skin on the back of his neck and gently shaking as you push him to the floor. Use the deep-throated, "NO!" or a loud yell as you correct him. Never pick him up by the scruff of the neck as this can cause injury to any size dog.

Formal Training

When your puppy is about six months old he will be ready for a puppy kindergarten class. By this time your puppy will be eager for a challenge and the two of you will be ready to take another step in your journey together. You will both feel proud as you progress to adult obedience class. As you gain more patience and expertise, these classes will provide tools with which to channel your unique dog's energy and develop his unique Scottie personality. Your classes should be chosen with care, however. Look for trainers who have developed gentle techniques and never accept harsh discipline which breaks your Scottie's spirit.

Conclusion

You have chosen a unique dog to share your home and heart. The Scottie spirit, while mischievous and beguiling, can be a real challenge, living up to his nickname 'the diehard.' But patience and perseverence during his first year of training will result in a well-mannered Scottie which is undoubtedly one of the most wonderful of all God's creations.

Further Reading

This chapter is a revised version of three articles by Ginger McAfee published in *Great Scots Magazine*, "*Puppy Love: Tips on Choosing a Puppy,*" *GSM* Vol 1 No 4 (Jul/Aug) 1996; "*The Socialized Puppy: Terrier not Terror, Part 1,*" *GSM* Vol 1 No 6 (Nov/Dec) 1996; "*The Socialized Puppy: Terrier not Terror, Part 2,*" *GSM* Vol 2 No 1 (Jan/Feb) 1997.

On dominance and general control, see Nancy Baer and Steve Duno, *Leader of the Pack: How to Take Control of Your Relationship with Your Dog*. NY: Harper Paperbacks, 1996. On training, see Jeanne Carlson with Ranny Green, *Good Dogs, Bad Habits: The Complete A - to - Z Guide for Solving Your Dog's Behavior Problems*. NY: Fireside Books,1995; Dick Maller & Jeffrey Feinman, *21 Days to a Trained Dog*. NY: Fireside Books, 1977; The Monks of New Skete, *How To Be Your Dog's Best Friend: A Training Manual for Dog Owners*. Boston: Little, Brown & Company, 1978; Jack Volhard and Melissa Bartlett, *What All Good Dogs Should Know: The Sensible Way to Train*. NY: Howell Book House, 1991.

For an internalized perspective on animal behavior see Vicki Hearne, *Animal Happiness*. NY: Harper Perennial, 1995; Mordecai Siegal, *Understanding the Dog You Love: A Guide to Preventing and Solving Behavior Problems in Your Dog*. NY: Berkeley Books, 1994. For a humorous look at dog training see John T. Olson, *Too Proud to Beg: Self-Empowerment for Today's Dog*. Kansas City, MO: Andrews & McMeel, 1997; Ronnie Sellers, *The Official Dog Codependents Handbook*. Kennebunk, ME: Ronnie Sellers Productions, INC, 1997.

CHAPTER NINE

On Loving A 'Demon' Puppy

He never looked demonic. No horns or forked tail on this Caledonian charmer. In fact, Willie often looked downright angelic. But that is just like demons; they are crafty!

He came to us at four months of age, a golden boy full of Scottie piss and vinegar, and we soon invented our own theories as to the origins of the curious pair of matching white spots in his wheaten fur right at his shoulders. We told him that is where the Scottie Angels plucked his wings when they cast him out of Scottie heaven.

And cast him down they did, because our 'Wee Willie' was into everything and frustrated there was not more from the moment he arrived in our home. We added Willie, a.k.a. 'Sir William of Girard,' to our clan in October of 1996, joining our two Scotties, Nati, who was then a 9 year old female, and Gus, who was 7. Looking back on it now, it is clear the Scottie Angels wanted to teach all the 'old dogs' at our house new tricks! It was years since we dealt with puppy antics and our lives were sedate, and perhaps to those Scottie Angels above, even a bit stogy. Along came Willie and it was a whole new ball game.

'Stogy,' you see, was not a word in Willie's vocabulary. 'Rambunctious' was, and 'precocious,' and 'obstreperous!' In short— and his little legs were short— Willie was all Scottie, and we loved every inch of him!

Willie's first career in our home was as an 'ectomologist'— not the ordinary kinds who perform appendectomies and hemorrhoidectomies; Willie proved adept at fax-ectomies and carpet-ectomies. There are morals to be learned here, so let me explain.

The first sign that our Wee Willie was a precocious 'ectomologist' came on a day of especially dreadful snafus at the *Great Scots Magazine* office. It was a bad tech day from hell. The computer demons were in residence, and then suddenly the fax machine diabolically printed pages of hieroglyphics. It was publication deadline for the magazine and one of the writers was trying to fax her article from Seattle. I frantically operated on the fax machine and held my breath as my writer sent her magazine pages a third time.

'Wee Willie' at 16 weeks. Photo by Joseph Harvill

Perfect. I could read it. At last, one small triumph in a day of disasters.

You guessed it. Out of all the edibles Wee Willie could have snagged it was the prized success-at-last fax from Seattle he grabbed. It was three pages long, and his little legs were, well, lost in a shag carpet, so he took off streaking through the house, head thrown back like a running bull elk, the fax pages flapping over his head like a trophy! And talk about quick, that little guy was harder to grab than a greased piglet, and before anyone could rescue the fax, Willie had performed a major 'fax-ectomy' on it, leaving a gnarled ghost of its original form minus a gaping extraction which looked more like day old macaroni than a piece of the original fax!

Moral #1: *If thou canst not afford to lose it, puppy-proof it or weep.*

We installed 'child-proof' gates and Wee Willie was banned from the *GSM* office after the fax-ectomy.

But our Willie was just getting started.

I was engrossed at the computer in our home office one evening and my wife was wholly absorbed in balancing business accounts at the kitchen table. Herein is **Moral #2**: *He who engrosseth and loseth sight of his Scottie puppy contributeth to mischief.*

Now I do not know your style when you are in the midst of a creative surge, but for me it is focused concentration. I tune out all except my muse and let the thoughts and words fly.

Well, I was in one of those don't-bother-me-now-the-juices-are-flowing moods when the first inklings of the noise reached my tunnel-visioned brain.

"Skr-r-r-r-rip. Skrip. Skrip."

I did not really notice the sound at first, and only gradually did it force its way into my concentration.

"Skr-r-r-r-r-r-r-rip." Then silence. "Oh, it's nothing," I told myself. "Back to work!"

"Skr-r-r-r-r-r-r-r-r-r-r-r-rip!"

Somewhere deep in the synapses of my brain a belated alarm went off. A still small inner voice said, "Do you know where your 'kid' is tonight?"

I jumped up and headed for the noise, homing in on the sound through the house like a guided missle.

There was Willie sitting in the middle of the living room floor with a look on his up-turned face that said, "Hey, Dad. You won't believe what these strings of yarn in the berber carpet can do when you pull one real hard!"

In front of him in the middle of the room was a pile of gummed carpet yarn and a bald spot in the carpet the size of a plate.

Dad went nuts at that point, saying words he did not learn at seminary.

Enter Mom on Dad's heels— calming spirit that she is in our household— who said, "I think we just found a great spot for one of our colorful Indian rugs as an accent piece."

Moral #3: *When thy Scottie puppy giveth thee lemons, learn to make thine own lemonade.*

But our Wee Willie turned out to be more than an ectomologist. In fact, I came to suspect he was directly related to Alex Haley. At least Willie shared Haley's obsession with digging up one's 'roots.'

I knew Willie had amazing digging genes the first time I tried to hide his squeaky toy under my leg while playing together on the floor. One whiff of the toy's location and Willie sprang into his fast-forward-dig-'em-out-of-there mode faster than you can say "Ouch!" His little front legs went to work with enough speed and purpose to make an Intel computer chip go into meltdown. I knew right then this little guy was an archaeologist!

So I was not surprised to discover one day that the side portion of our backyard had turned into a suitable place for NASA's moonscape training. We had dandy craters around the perimeter of the enclosed area, two in the center, and another two behind the fir tree in the back.

Closer inspection, however, revealed the prize dig, the *sine qua non*, of Willie's budding archaeological career. Near the concrete block wall was a shoulder-high shrub which apparently had roots possessing mystical powers. I cannot swear to the powers, but no doubt Willie could. He excavated the roots and tendrils as fastidiously as a Harvard archaeologist seeking tenure.

Poor defenseless shrub.

I tried to work on being calm and to practice my skills in seeing the glass of life half-full rather than half-empty. After all, these dogs were bred to go to ground, and Willie was merely doing what comes naturally. Furthermore that side portion of the yard was fallow space we set aside for just such a contingency. Nevertheless, I am having nightmares about Shrubbery Rights Activists with hostile faces suing me blind in Judge Judy's court!

Moral #4: *He who ignoreth Mother Nature payeth a price.*

And our battles against the puppy demons went beyond struggles against Wee Willie's flagrant 'deconstructionism.' We waged a holy war in the cause of house-training. I despaired Willie would ever get it. A perpetual clean-up rag and bucket of vinegar water stayed in the kitchen to neutralize the amonia scent of Willie's accidents. The only thing the vinegar water accomplished was to make me self-conscious when I was up-wind of people in public places.

But we struggled on— to save our faxes, to hide our prematurely balding berber carpet, to save a shrub, and to rise above our embarrassment in crowds ("Why are you staring? We're pickling cucumbers at home!").

We took refuge in the counsel of a wise Scottie lover who reassured us: "The more intelligent the Scottie, the more difficult to train."

Ah, the joys of the gifted. We were certain we had adopted MacEinstein.

Our re-education, of course, was in matters which time and forgetfulness erase, viz., that raising a puppy is a lot of work, and it is a lot of work *all* the time. It was our lapses, not Willie's, which led to grief. Pup-parenting is not a task you can relegate to the back burner— unless you want to catch your house on fire! Raising MacJunior is white water all the way and survival depends a great deal on your vigilance, your planning, and your attitude when negotiating the hazards.

And that brings up the last of the morals our Wee Willie taught us. When we moved to Albuquerque a year and a half before acquiring Willie the berber carpet was showing some wear and we debated whether to replace it. But our guardian angel smiled on us. We reasoned that since we were contemplating adding a puppy to our family we ought to wait on new floors— like maybe six years! We knew if you can't afford to lose it, don't have it around.

It does not take a genius to guess how glad we are now we did not put down new berber carpet. And that is **Moral #5**: *He who wanteth a Scottie puppy must love the dog more than he loveth the 'things' which MacJunior destroyeth!*

Looking back on it, I would not trade a single minute of Willie's puppyhood. Like all good things, it was over before we knew it. Today the demons are gone— at least, most of them. Willie just turned four, and he has matured into a handsome, regal Scot, adding his own unique charm and considerable dignity to our family. He is my 'Shaker dog' because, like the early religious group by that name, he loves to spin-and-twirl when he is excited.

Willie has taught me that the Scottie good life is about celebration. It is about making memories and soul-making, about sharing the shadows as well as the sunshine which blend in life to make matters of the heart. As Nati always spoke to my intellect, and Gus to my contemplative side, so Willie now speaks to my inner-child with all the welcome exuberance of the young just discovering the joys of the good life shared.

Scottie puppies, I have learned, are not for the faint of heart. But then, neither is love.

'Wee Willie' as he is today, "a handsome, regal Scot, adding his own unique charm to our family." Photo by J. Harvill.

Further Reading

This chapter is a revised version of three articles that appeared under the title, *"Willie Watch,"* by Joseph Harvill, Ph.D., in *GSM* Vol 2 No 1 (Jan/Feb) 1997, *GSM* Vol 2 No 2 (Mar/Apr) 1997, *GSM* Vol 3 No 1 (Jan/Feb) 1998.

For further reading on puppies, training, and socialization see the bibliography in chaps. seven and eight.

CHAPTER TEN

... And Baby Makes Four: A Case Study

Deborah Balcom and Joseph Harvill

On a beautiful September day last fall, we were blessed with the birth of our precious daughter Rebecca Lynn. She was long awaited by family, friends, and especially a little black Scottie named Jack, known affectionately in our home as "Little Buddy." You see, Little Buddy knew something very different was happening.

For nine months he waited right at our sides. He was my constant companion as morning sickness lingered five months. He enjoyed the extra snuggles on the couch brought on by my exhaustion with a growing baby. Morning and nightly walks to keep mom in shape suited him perfectly. And perhaps best of all, he loved the extra visits from Nana and Poppop, the proud grandparents-to-be, who stopped by the house often.

On the special day we went to the hospital at 6 A.M. The grandparents hurried over to the house to care for Jack while Rebecca hurried into the world by Casarean. Our dreams had come true: a healthy, beautiful daughter had joined our family.

Jack patiently waited for us all to return with our little surprise to add to his pack. Days passed with sniffs and looks as Jack got used to his new sister and friend. At first he scarcely noticed Rebecca, until one day she started crying in the bassinet and he went crazy barking to let us know she was there and needed help!

We noticed right away, however, that Rebecca was fascinated by Jack. She could see him from the start, because he was black! Her first giggles were over Jack's puppy ways. We all enjoyed watching their mutual friendship grow.

Today our lives are filled with baby smiles, family walks with stroller and leash in tow, treats dropped by Rebecca for the ever-hungry Jack, and all the wonders of a growing family. Now that Rebecca is crawling, we are always watching to keep her out of Jack's food and toys, and he out of hers. We trust Jack, but we understand that he needs his own space and time, so we respect his needs, and work always to teach Rebecca how to gently love and respect him, too.

The Lord blesses us all in so many ways. We are so thankful for our bundle of love named Rebecca, and for our furry bundle of love named Jack.

So when people ask us how many are in our family now, we pause and say, ". . . and baby makes four."

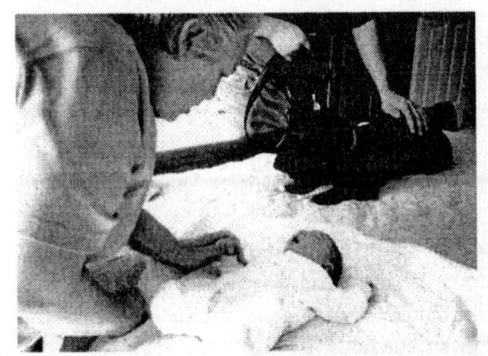

With a reassuring touch from dad, Jack, the 4 year-old Scottie in the Balcom family, meets Rebecca Balcom, four days old. Nana helps with the introductions. Photo by D. Balcom.

Nine month old Rebecca learns to be gentle with Jack by practicing "nice petting" under dad's supervision. Photo by D. Balcom.

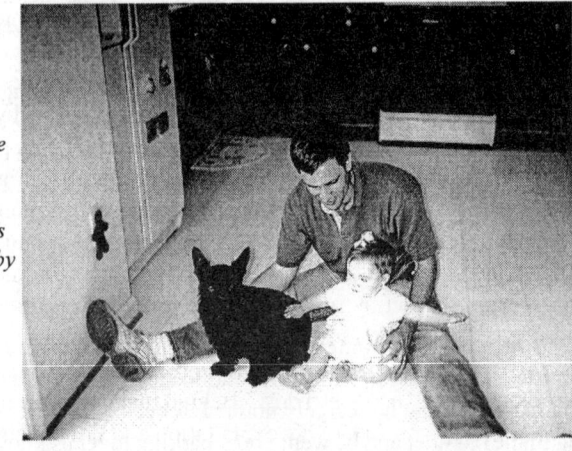

Scotties and Babies
A Case Study: The Balcom Family
Joseph Harvill

The popular stereotype is: Scotties and children do not mix. However, it is my conviction that Scotties are no more dysfunctional than humans when it comes to family relations. The truth about this Scottie stereotype and every other is: *it all depends*— it depends on genetics, it depends on particulars of environment, it depends on precise socialization. It all depends.

Because this negative stereotype of Scotties is so pervasive it is worthwhile to look closely at the Balcom family model in order to tease out the variables in their case which contribute to their success and which show why the almost categorical bad press given Scotties and children is inaccurate and should be corrected by those who know and love Scotties.

The Problem

As everyone knows who is intimately acquainted with our breed, Scotties have a deep and rich sense of themselves. Scotties are sometimes more 'people' than people. That is not a flaw, except to the insecure. It is precisely this sense-of-self which makes possible the profound bonds of companionship which are normative among Scottie lovers; these dogs can become friends in a sense quite remarkable.

It is this great dignity and sense-of-self which also makes Scotties terribly unsuited to be furniture or yard ornaments in a family. I believe being treated as chattal violates a Scottie's psyche in ways that parallel experiences of de-humanization in persons.

It is when Scotties are 'de-Scottie-fied' that problems arise. Here is the root of the bad reputation which clings to Scotties *vis-a-vis* children.

My hunch is the bad-with-children scenario goes something like this: new Scottie owners acquire their dog attracted more by the cute bug than a relational impulse to bond with a friend; Scottie's rich personality ensconces him as 'the child' at the center of his new family; all goes well until a new human baby arrives, at which time Scottie is unceremoniously and overnight stripped of his centrality and relegated to furniture status, along with the bassinet and stroller; Scottie reacts by trying to protect his role in the pack; the new parents react by sending Scottie to the animal shelter, mom saying, "I can't have our child at risk!"

Where is the fault here? Bad dog? I think not. The real culprit here is the hidden notion, "he's just a dog." Behind that phrase lie anthropocentric ignorance and hubris that justify exploitation and brutalization of all 'lesser' animals, including Scotties. Since he is "just a dog" he can be used or abused at will—and sent to the animal shelter when he is no longer convenient.

The uncomplimentary truth is, the cast-off Scottie may be better off, since he may be fortunate enough to be adopted by persons who will relate to him as a friend rather than as excess furniture.

But it is the success of a family such as the Balcoms which reminds us that Scotties and children can mix; that when Scotties are treated as true companions and not wallpaper they are no more dysfunctional than others in the family and can greatly enrich the bonds of family love.

The Balcom Model

From interviews with the Balcoms at least five important keys emerge as guideposts for successfully integrating Scotties with new children.

1. **Preparation**. The Balcom case shows they started early preparing themselves and their Scottie, Jack, for the new arrival. Starting early with the mental preparation to anticipate reactions and outcomes and to think through strategies is not only the right way to successfully introduce a Scottie and a new baby, it is the sensible way to prepare every family member for the changes a new baby brings! The point is: do not leave out Scottie in the preparation; he is part of the family who will be impacted by the new arrival. Realize this and take steps to compensate.

2. **Respect and Reciprocity**. As the Balcom photos indicate, they are teaching mutual respect to both Jack and their new infant from day one. Jack must learn to respect and love the baby, but the child must learn to love and respect the Scottie 'sibling' too. Each must be disciplined to behave in ways that affirm mutual respect and caring. Discipline does not have to be harsh to be effective, but it does have to be consistent and reciprocal: the family rule must be that respect is double-edged; to be respected you must be respectful.

3. **Empathy**. The Balcom case reveals exemplary inclusive thinking. They do not leave Jack out of their lives but include him in their evolving family. This is nothing revolutionary; it is what one does with one's friends and family—they are part of the package of our world and they ought to be sensitively included in our planning.

Empathy, which is the mental and emotional practice of putting oneself in another's place, of looking at situations through another's eyes, is the Balcom's long-suit, and it is the virtue which most directly enhances the integration of children into Scottie households. Clearly Jack is not 'wallpaper' in the Balcom home; his needs and presence are thoughtfully taken into account as part of the family. In a phone interview Deborah explained how she and her husband dealt with the first few nights of the baby's arrival. Jack always slept with the Balcoms. However, Deborah felt that since the baby was nursing it was preferrable for the baby to sleep with mom alone for the first few nights. To prepare for this change in the family's routine, dad slept with Jack in the

Scottie, 'Jock MacBender,' of Tacoma, WA., helps out swimming buddy, Gabriella, with a kiss. Scotties and children CAN mix unforgettably. Photo by Mrs. Walter Bender.

guest room for a week before the baby was due to facilitate mom and new baby working out their feeding schedule once Rebecca came home.

Such heads-up, thoughtful sensitivity to their Scottie's potential sense of displacement goes a long way toward explaining the Balcom's success in nurturing their family.

4. **Positivity**. A glance at the photos accompanying the Balcom story (p. 78) shows the positive tone manifest in their household. Look at their faces: they are blessed, and it shows. I cannot overemphasize the importance of the psychological and relational tone or climate in a family as a factor in the quality of any integration attempt involving Scotties— or humans, for that matter.

There *is* such a thing as self-fulfilling prophecy, and I believe our dogs mirror in important ways the spirit and perspectives of the environment in which they live. Neurotic people foster neurotic dogs. Aggressive people, aggressive dogs. Happy people, happy dogs.

The unwelcome truth here lurks just below the surface: since every family is dysfunctional in some sense (after all, there are no perfect people, so there are no perfect families!), our Scotties share in our flawed family circles. But it is manifestly simplistic to blame the dog if family life is less than ideal. The point is our families, including Scotties, are complex, reflexive systems all the parts of which contribute to both problems and solutions. Establishing and nourishing a positive rather than distrustful family environment goes a long way towards promoting bonding and harmony among all involved.

5. **Pace**. Finally, the Balcom case shows they see the integration of their family as a long-term goal. They practice slow guidance, taking baby steps in their training of both Rebecca and Jack. They know relationships are built over time, not created by edict. Just as their committment to Rebecca is for life, so too their committment to Jack is not interim—until they have children!— but is for the duration. I believe Jack knows this, too. And when a Scottie is loved and respected as friend and family, he reciprocates with great-souled devotion to his family, whether infant or adult.

Conclusion

There are individuated variables, of course, of genetics, environment and socialization, the permutations of which make it impossible to generalize across the breed as to how individual Scotties will relate to children. It all depends.

However, the Balcom model showing preparation/planning, respect and mutuality, empathy, positivity, and pace, points the way to successful integration of Scotties and children. It is not so impossible after all. The secret is doing the things necessary to become a functional family in the first place!

Brainerd, MN., Scottie, 'Aryn,' shares naptime with ragdoll Annie and 7 year-old Abijah at grandmother's home. Photo: Mrs. Brenda DeWitt.

Further Reading

This material first appeared as accompanying articles, *"... And Baby Makes Four,"* by Deborah Balcom, and *"Scotties and Babies: A Case Study— The Balcom Family,"* by Joseph Harvill, in *GSM* Vol 4 No 5 (Sep/Oct) 1999.

CHAPTER ELEVEN

Shortcourse In Walking the Dog

Lee Netzler

The first time I took my new Scottie puppy for a walk it seemed a very natural and simple thing to do. Now, after thousands of dog walks, although it still feels natural, I know that doing it right is not as simple as it looks.

Looking back I can remember many times when, through my ignorance, I exposed my dogs to danger. I did not realize, for example, that letting my dog explore prairie dog (or other varmint) holes without restraint exposed it to mites, fleas and other parasites, and could even bring the dog into contact with deadly bubonic plague bacteria. Another time I briefly allowed my dog to trot out of sight while hiking and it wandered alone down a very narrow section of trail where the sheer drop-off was measured in hundreds of feet. In another hiking situation I let the dog out of my sight for a few seconds and it came face to face with a young marmot— a harmless creature, but the encounter easily could have been with a more dangerous animal. And, in my most idle-minded moment, I let my off-lead dog get beyond voice control where it strayed well within striking distance of a coiled rattlesnake!

I confess at one time or another as I was learning I made nearly every mistake possible. While I have been lucky to escape the disasters my ignorance deserved, I am left with reverent appreciation of my good fortune and a firm determination not to rely on dumb luck. For the sake of our dogs I want to help other dog-walkers to avoid my mistakes by sharing a shortcourse in walking ettiquette.

Risks

My advice can be summed up in one statement: a responsible person out for a dog-walk always keeps two things in mind— safety and health. Safety is the first concern and it includes both the safety of your Scottie and the safety of others who may come in contact with your dog. Concern for health is equally important, and likewise, it includes the health of your dog, other animals, other people, and your own health, too.

The dangers are many— from dog bites (given or received), bites from other creatures, injuries from sharp objects or falls, exposure to heat exhaustion, to freezing, or drowning, contact with poisons, parasites, giardia, rabies, harmful organisms— and on and on. We cannot, of course, be prepared for every possible threat, but we can prepare for most everything by following a few guidelines that apply whether we are taking a walk around the block, in a park, along a beach, or hiking through a desert, a forest or a remote wilderness area.

Rules

Tags. First of all *your dog should carry identification*. The most common heartbreak for dog owners is a lost dog. Do not let it happen to you. At a minimum, your Scottie needs a secure collar with identification tags firmly attached.

Control. The second guideline is *keep your dog under control*. Limiting how much your dog is able to become involved with the new environment gives you substantial control over any risks present. The best method of control is to keep the dog on a

Staying in control of your Scottie precludes surprises that could spell trouble. Shown here is Lee Netzler and his Scottie, Rusty.

leash. The standard six foot training lead is an excellent choice and works well everywhere. Longer leads or retractable leads may also do the job in less confined areas while allowing more freedom. The ability of the handler to effectively control the dog and to protect it from an unexpected danger should determine the length of the lead.

If you intend to permit your dog off lead it must always obey, regardless of distractions, at least two commands:

♦ "WAIT" — a verbal command for the dog to stop in place and to remain there motionless until the handler goes to the dog and grasps the collar;

♦ "COME" — a verbal command for the dog to return immediately to the handler and to permit the handler to grasp the collar.

The 'Wait' command could have made the difference between life and death when my dog encountered the rattlesnake. It could also save your dog's life when it is about to run into the street. The 'Come' command can bring your dog back to you faster than you can go to your dog. And it allows you to quickly reattach the lead when circumstances change and trouble threatens. If your Scottie is not trained to respond, without fail, to these two commands, then keep it on lead at all times.

Years ago the paperboy, who had previously played with my Scottie many, many times, reached inside our unlocked screen door to pet the dog and was promptly bitten on the finger. When I think about how that seemingly harmless unlocked screen at home— a small loss of control— resulted in a dog bite, it makes me consider all the more seriously how a loss of control in a public place is magnified and could be so much more threatening.

Knowledge. My third guideline is to *know the rules of the area where you are walking and honor them*. By doing so you will have an idea of what situations to expect and you can plan for those situations. Most cities, for example, require a dog to wear a dog license tag, a proof of rabies vaccination tag, and to be kept on a six foot leash. Seeing a loose dog in a city, especially

"Public access for you and your Scottie should not be taken for granted. Let's save what's left by our good manners, our good examples, and especially by our good dogs." The author explores a mountain lake with Rusty in Colorado.

one without collar and tags, usually means the dog is not under control and could pose a threat to you or your dog. Beware and be ready.

In some places, such as county Open Space areas, dogs are permitted off leash. While you may not choose to let your dog off lead, it is important for you to know that you may encounter other unrestrained dogs who may be aggressive or who may provoke your Scottie to react and to become physically protective. In locations where dogs are used for hunting, for example, you are almost certain to encounter dogs who are large, nosey, and almost always running free. Expect them to fearlessly trot right up to you and to start sniffing at your dog. Know the rules before you start walking in an area so you can either prepare yourself and your dog accordingly, or else avoid that area.

Yield. My fourth guideline is, *yield the path to others*. This rule is more than good manners; it is also an effective way to avoid unpredictable situations that are potentially explosive. If your dog has never met a llama on the trail, for example, standing too close as it passes could produce surprises that you, the dog, the llama and the llama's owner never expected and wished afterwards had been avoided.

My point is do not give the unexpected an opportunity to happen. I have seen a dog who was raised with horses suddenly yip and snap when he met an unfamiliar mare on the trail. The kick and buck which followed were real surprises to everyone, and although the incident ended without harm, it could have ended with serious consequences and sad regrets.

So get out of the way and give plenty of room to that friendly looking pooch coming down the sidewalk toward you. Otherwise you may be painfully surprised to discover that it snaps and bites at other dogs whether big or little, white or black, long-haired or whatever. And never believe the owner who says, "Oh, my dog won't bite." Believe me, in the right circumstances, it will.

Clean up. Guideline five is, *pick up after your dog*. Yes, that's right—pick up after your dog! Not only is this good manners, it is a health issue. I really do not want my dog nosing some other dog's droppings. I do not want the risk of infection and sickness that can lurk there, either for the sake of my Scottie's health or my own, nor do I want to endure the sufferings that illness brings, or the high cost of veterinary bills to treat them. You do not want these hazards either. So do us all a favor and pick up after your dog.

Example. That brings me to the sixth and last guideline— *protect our access to public places by practicing good manners*. If you create a mess and do not clean it up, or your dog is threatening and aggressive, or you are involved in a dog bite or a dog fight incident, you are jeopardizing our future access to public places. It is virtually impossible, for example, to enforce park ordinances which require owners to pick up after their dogs, but it is easy and effective for city councils to simply ban dogs from parks. Look around. You will see countless examples where irresponsible dog woners have ruined it for all dogs. Public access for you and your Scottie should not be taken for granted. Let us save what is left by our good manners, our good examples, and especially by our good dogs.

Conclusion

For Scottie lovers a walk with your Scottie companion is one of life's special pleasures. Any day that I can share a pleasant walk with my Scottie is a good day for me. Follow these guidelines and if by chance we meet someday on the sidewalk or the trail, I know it will be a good day for both of us.

Further Reading

This chapter was published originally as, *"Just A-Walkin' the Dog: Shortcourse in Ettiquette,"* by Lee Netzler, in *GSM* Vol 2 No 1 (Jan/Feb) 1997.

For detailed information on snake-bite see *"Snake-Bite: These Wagging Tails Mean Trouble,"* by Joseph Harvill, Ph.D., *GSM* Vol 2 No 2 (Mar/Apr) 1997.

For motivation and strategy for developing good habits of picking up after your dog, see the ***Great Scots Magazine*** article which won the Dog Writers Association of America's top award for 'Best Article in a Single Breed Magazine' for 1999, *"The Scoop On Poop,"* by Joseph Harvill, *GSM* Vol 4 No 3 (May/Jun) 1999.

*Lee Netzler and Rusty in their home state of Colorado. Lee is a retired air-traffic controller, Scottie poet, freelance writer, and staff writer for **Great Scots Magazine**.*

CHAPTER TWELVE

Eleven Rules for Growing Old Scottily

Bonnie Wee McNati, a.k.a. Nati
as told to and illustrated by Joseph Harvill

---

rule #1

Greet each day with hope and expectation, wipe from memory any hurt or slight from yesterday. Every dog has his day. Make this one yours.

Eleven Rules 89

rule #2

Be affectionate. Never restrain your love since your loved ones thrive on it. Remember: you are not the cat.

rule #3

Self-Whelp Tip:

The good life is about love not length.

Love hard. Life is short.

rule #4

Always make time to play.

rule #5

Be still and know that you are DOG. Find your center. Adjust your position until you are comfortable and nap, nap, nap.

Eleven Rules 91

rule #6

Know when to bark, when to yelp, when to whine, and above all, know when to be quiet.

rule #7

Try to behave. But don't miss a run at pigeons now and then just for fun.

rule #8

Remember: share the quiet with someone you love.

rule #9

Express yourself.

Sometimes you just have to yip, bark, and howl to rid your soul of its demons.

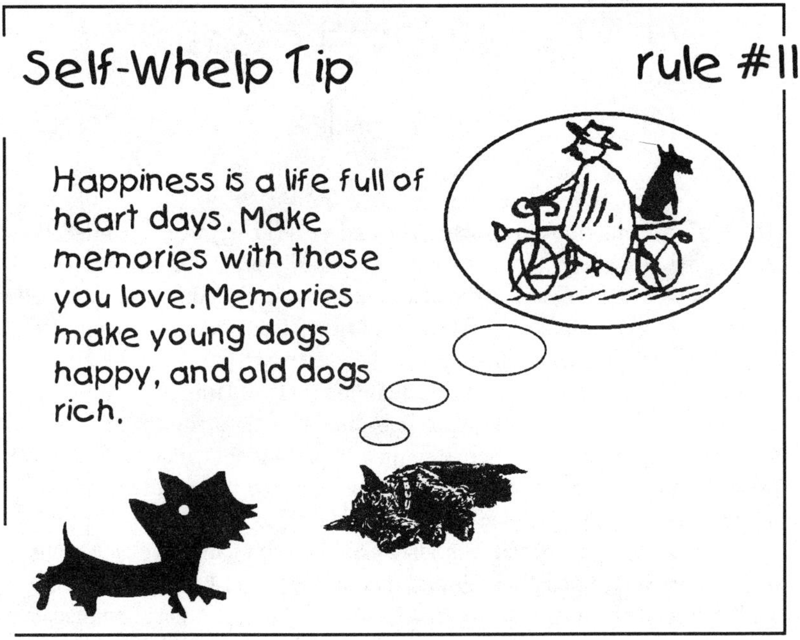

rule #10

Make 'scents' of your world. Sniff. Sniff. Sniff. Stay informed. Forget speed reading. Savor life's good stuff!

Self-Whelp Tip

rule #11

Happiness is a life full of heart days. Make memories with those you love. Memories make young dogs happy, and old dogs rich.

Further Reading

This chapter appeared as, *"Dogmas: Eleven Rules for Growing Old Scottily"* in ***GSM*** Vol 4 No 3 (May/Jun) 1999. 'Bonnie Wee McNati,' the little Scottie who inspired ***Great Scots Magazine***, died in Albuquerque, NM., February 1999 at 12 years of age. See an extensive tribute to 'Miss Nati' written by Joseph Harvill in that same issue.

CHAPTER THIRTEEN

Each Day A Victory: Living with Scottie Cancer

Marki Shalloe

Seamus looked up at me, cocking his head to gauge my mood. When satisfied that I was neither unusually cranky nor half asleep, he burst forward, grabbed the toe of my fuzzy bedroom slipper, pulled it off my foot, and took off. The rest of us — husband Kevin, thick-lashed Scottie Finola Frances, long-legged Schnauzer Gretchen, and one-shoed me — took off in hot pursuit. After several minutes of wild running, we collapsed, giggling, Seamus tossing the slipper in the air with a triumphant "Arooo!" signaling victory over his inferior competitors. "Arooo!" indeed. Two weeks prior, we had not counted on Seamus being with us by now, much less leading us around tables and chairs at Scottie warp-speed.

On May 17th, our vet diagnosed Seamus with a massive cancerous tumor encroaching upon two-thirds of his bladder. We had three options, he said. Surgery, chemotherapy, or simply doing nothing. Surgery sounded complex; they would have to remove his entire bladder, rerouting his urine through his bowel. "He would be totally incontinent," our vet said gently. "It would be very difficult to live with a dog like that." No, no ... we could live with incontinence. What was a ruined floor when compared to the loss of our beloved Seamie? Unfortunately, calls to veterinary colleges confirmed the seriousness of this operation. Many dogs do not survive it; when they told us of

Seamus Shalloe, "the bladder cancer warrior," sits in his favorite quiet place in his yard in Marietta, GA. Despite a shaved coat on his side and back, Seamus' Scottie spirit has been undaunted by intensive cancer therapy. Photo by M. Shalloe.

the two week hospital stay it would involve, we shook our head "No." For many dogs with less massive tumors, surgery may be viable.

For us, the risks appeared to far outweigh the slight hope it provided. We discussed chemotherapy, which our vet had never administered for bladder cancer, but researched valiantly on his own time. A new drug, Piroxicam, seemed promising, but he would need to know more about it before he could give us a recommendation. Chemotherapy? We had held hands with human friends undergoing chemotherapy and watched them lose their appetite, their energy, and their hair. How could we do this to our baby? Worst of all, chemotherapy would not cure him, it would just put off our loss.

After hearing the options, it seemed kinder to Seamus to do nothing. Utterly devastated, we posed the hardest question: How long do we have? With surgery or chemotherapy, six months to a year. Without it, eventually the tumor would totally encompass his bladder and he would be unable to urinate. At the rate this malignancy was growing, perhaps less than a month.

When we got home, my husband went to the calendar and wrote "Seamus dying" on the box for Monday, May 17th. His Irish heritage then compelled him to the bedroom to mourn his dear friend for the remainder of the day.

Downstairs, I held Seamus and tried to make bargains with God. My sister, the devoted Catholic, sent a medal for the patron saint of cancer, which we dutifully put on Seamus' collar. Tuesday, May 18th, I cried at work for the first time in sixteen years.

By Wednesday, I could not stand it any longer. If my family was attacked by a bear, would I sit back and let it happen? If someone waved a gun at me, would I say, Okay, it is God's will? Wednesday was my pivotal day, the day I hope you have should you have to deal with significant illness.

My pivotal day changed my attitude from devastated acceptance to a furious need to wage war on this illness. I went to the calendar, erased "Seamus dying" and wrote in "Seamus *challenged*." I then went to the phone book and called the only animal internist listed. Surprisingly, he called me back within an hour. "Don't give up," he said. "There are real options and chemotherapy may be a good one." Oh, boy. Real options! This was enough to get my husband out of the bedroom and both of us to an appointment with the internist. I was uncomfortable asking my regular vet for Seamus' file, but all is fair in love and war ... and this was both.

The internist first assured us he had administered chemotherapy for this illness many times. Unlike people, animals almost always tolerate chemotherapy well. If Seamus does not, he promisesd, we could always take him off it with no damage. He confirmed that this was no cure, but said he had often seen months added to dogs' lives and the quality of their life improved. That day, we started Seamus on Mitoxantrone given every three weeks. As my original vet's research suggested, Piroxicam, an anti-inflammatory used for human arthritis patients, helped many animals by dramatically lessening straining and blood during urination. We give Seamie 5 mg every other day. The internist also suggested bolstering Seamus' immune system by changing his diet to high protein and high fat, reducing carbohydrates. We gradually introduced Seamus to Hill's Prescription Diet N/D™ canned food, which we supplement with chicken and "Scottage cheese." Many nights, Seamie gets steak while we eat hamburger! Each day, we also give him Cell Forte (from the vet), 200 IU of vitamin E, 500 mg Vitamin C with bioflavonoids, 25,000 units of Vitamin A and two cloves of garlic (we eat it too so we will all be stinky!).

We found we had to be diligent about costs. Everything Seamus is getting except the chemotherapy is a human prescription obtained from a regular drugstore. By calling every pharmacy in the phone book, I discovered that a one-month prescription for 10 mg Piroxicam varied in price from $53.00 (Feldene) to $5.99 (generic). Per the many pharmacists I spoke to, the generic is identical. Prices for the generic were highest at CVS ($17.00) and lowest at Eckerd ($5.99). Most discount stores such as Wal-Mart and Kmart were in the $7.00 range. Cell Forte I got from our internist, but A, C, and E were over-the-counter people vitamins. Keep trying until you find the best price in the best form (don't buy vitamin A in units of 1,000 if your dog needs 25,000 units or you'll be poking pills down your poor Scottie all day). We have found the gelcaps to be easiest to administer, particularly as most of the vitamins and medicines must be given with food.

You can also affect the price of veterinary care. A sonogram at our regular vet cost $230, while a subsequent sonogram at our internist's cost $75. When asked about the difference, our vet explained that because they did not have sonogram equipment, they had to call in a mobile sonogram provider. My vet is honorable and charges nothing extra for these sonograms; however, the cost of these journeyman tests are extreme. Had we taken our Scottie to a specialist at the first hint of this illness, the tests involved would have been much cheaper. Many tests performed at our regular vet's had to be augmented or redone as they were not comprehensive enough (for example, though we had X-rays of the urinary tract, no X-rays were done of the chest area so we did not know if the cancer had spread).

Overall, the initial internist exam, blood tests, biopsy, x-rays, and chemotherapy cost $450 (this included the Cellular Forte prescription and the canned food). In June, we expect the chemo to cost less as the initial testing is complete; however, as Seamus also had prior parathyroid and calcium deficiency problems, continual blood testing will increase the cost for us. Chemotherapy by itself was $112.00.

As you fight your war, remember you have allies. One of the first things I did was email everyone with a Scottie web page on the Internet, asking them what they knew about bladder cancer. The response was tremendous. One particularly wonderful warrior (the mother of Fala Pink and Sky Blue) sent my email to 700 breeders. Those who did not have medical advice had good wishes. Readers of *Great Scots Magazine* were marvelous, suggesting medical websites and, most importantly, sending me emails about their "challenged" Scotties who are still alive and Arooo-ing months after diagnosis (for example, Josh, diagnosed with 95% of his bladder affected at the end of 1998, is still Arooo-ing away). Add me to your ally list: kevinob@mindspring.com, or for the snail-mailers, Marki Shalloe at 483 Salem Woods Drive, Marietta, GA 30067.

It is now May 29th. We have had bad days, in which Seamus had to be begged to eat, and great days (such as the Grand Slipper-Chase). At first, Seamus ate well after chemotherapy. We have learned by trial and error that his later avoidance of food is linked to his distrust of the medicine in it, rather than chemo-induced nausea. We now put his medicine in small bites of his most beloved treats, rather than in his regular meals, so he is learning again to trust his food bowl. (Remember to feed your Scottie immediately after many medicines to avoid nausea.) If we are lucky, we will have one more year with our Seamus. We truly feel we have been blessed with this extra time.

Unfortunately, more and more Scotties are being diagnosed with cancer at Seamus' age (ten years). I wish I could tell you there is a cure, but I cannot.

If your Scottie is one of the "challenged," however, take heart in the fact that there are options. No matter how much you trust your veterinarian, if they do not regularly administer chemotherapy (or perform surgery) for this disease, find someone that does. Your costs will decrease and you will have the comfort of knowing that the person responsible for your Scottie's care knows all the ins and outs. Keep your regular vet involved in the care as well due to your vet's history with the dog. It is a combination of General Practitioner and specialist that works best.

Research everything, but remember to check out anything you find with a veterinarian you trust. Call on others with the same challenge who will share information. Above all, treasure every day with your Scottie (even if it means getting a new pair of slippers). Do not lose heart. Believe in your Scottie. Remember Mark Twain's words: "Heaven goes by favor. If it went by merit, you'd stay out and your dog would go in."

Summary On Bladder Cancer

Here is a cheat sheet for this illness. Obviously, I am no vet and every dog is different, so be sure to have a trusted doctor check everything you plan to do.

TRANSITIONAL CELL CARCINOMA, BLADDER

♦ Have an ultrasound performed every year once your Scottie begins to age. If we had done this, we would have caught this tumor while it was much more manageable.

♦ See a specialist. Even if you decide to have your regular vet control your Scottie's care, a second opinion will confirm your options and make you feel better. Don't feel uncomfortable about this. My regular vet is extraordinary, but if you were going to have brain surgery, who would you go to, a brain surgeon or your G.P.?

♦ For us, Mitoxantrone has been a good option. Seamus has been pretty normal and we have hope that this will help shrink the tumor. Remember, this isn't a cure, but it may buy you some quality time.

♦ Everything I've heard about Piroxicam is positive, with no ill effects on the dog. Even if you decide against chemotherapy, Piroxicam by itself seems like a good option. Pardon me for repeating myself, but ask your vet.

♦ Try to boost your Scottie's immune system with a high protein diet, low carbohydrates, and vitamins A, C, and E. Natural garlic has been tough to get Seamus to eat, so we are considering capsules.

♦ Remember that putting medicine in your dog's food may make your Scottie distrust it. Don't automatically assume nausea from chemotherapy if your Scottie isn't eating. It might just take some patience to get your Scottie comfortable with his meals.

♦ Have x-rays done to ensure the disease hasn't spread before you decide on any treatment option.

We started this process when we found a little bit of blood in Seamus' urine (it showed up on a nighttime wee-wee pad and was almost undetectable). We treated him with antibiotics for two weeks, believing he had a urinary infection, then a minor stone. It was only after we saw a massive amount of blood that the vet performed the first ultrasound. Blood in Scottie's urine is a big red flag for this disease. Insist upon an ultrasound immediately if you have any idea there may be blood in the urine.

As I come across new treatment options, I will write *Great Scots Magazine* and hope that other readers will do the same. I hear a researcher is working on a treatment that will block the flow of blood to tumors, starving them out. We are watching her work closely. New treatments are popping up all the time. Do not give up hope.

Further Reading

Marki Shalloe is a commercial real estate financier living with husband, Kevin, Scotties and an adopted Schnauzer in Marietta, GA. Marki is a freelance writer and published playwrite. Despite the family's best efforts and Seamus' remarkable 'diehard' spirit, Seamus lost his battle against bladder cancer in December of 1999. Marki's triumphant attitude and refusal to give up before it was time is a model for Scottie lovers battling this disease. Scotties remain 18 times more likely to have bladder cancer than other breeds. New cancer research at Purdue University may at last offer explanation and hope.

This chapter first appeared in *GSM*, Vol 4 No 4 (Jul/Aug) 1999.

For more information on Scotties and bladder cancer see "*Glad You Asked About New Bladder Cancer Test*," by Marcia Dawson, D.V.M., *GSM*, Vol 5 No 3 (May/Jun) 2000, and "*Death Takes a Holiday: Scottie Lover Finds New Weapon to Fight Bladder Cancer*," by Karen Williams, *GSM*, Vol 5 No 4 (Jul/Aug) 2000. See also the excellent health information center at 'ScottiePhile' the catalog of health-related articles sponsored by the Scottish Terrier Club of America @ http://www.akc.org/clubs/stca/index.html.

CHAPTER FOURTEEN

The Art of Loving Well

He battled cancer for 15 months. "*How will we know when it's his time?*" his anxious owners asked the vets at the University of Minnesota Veterinary Teaching Hospital. "*You'll know,*" they comforted. "*He'll let you know.*"

On the morning of June 3, 1996— the day scheduled for a phone interview with Elizabeth and Stephen Buckingham about coping with Scottie terminal illness— Argyle Hopscotch Buckingham let his family know that he could not fight his canine lymphosarcoma any more. They bundled him up and took him to the Animal Hospital where he died quietly in their arms.

I called later that day at the scheduled hour unaware of the day's trauma at the Buckingham house, and was greeted by tearful but upbeat voices as the Buckinghams expressed their wishes to honor Argyle's spirit by pursuing the interview. Their desire was that their 15-month ordeal with death and dying be shared with other Scottie lovers as a legacy from Argyle, so that, though he is gone, the important lessons on how to love which were learned by the Buckinghams due to Argyle's terminal condition, might be remembered, shared, and multiplied.

Argyle was just a few days short of 9 years old when he died. 'Argy,' as the Buckinghams affectionately knew him, lived a full and wonderful life, and, like many Scotties I've known, was the centerpiece in a home without children where he gave and received unconditional love.

Argy was exceptional. A singer of eclectic tastes, his sing-a-longs ranged from Grateful Dead to grand opera. He loved to 'play ball,' often inventing his own games to amuse himself. He was affectionate and sociable, but like a true Scotsman, he knew quickly whom he liked and disliked. For nine wonderful years Argy and his owners knew the joy and intimacy of a shared bed and the deep bonds such companionship affords. But most of all, the last 15 months, stressful as they were with their terminal portent, Liz and Stephen and Argy learned to welcome each new day as a gift, to make memories, and to love well.

Argyle Hopscotch Buckingham at his home in Minnesota. Photo by Elizabeth Buckingham.

Legacy For Scottie Lovers

Out of our conversations, in which I asked them to share their experience and wisdom, I've gleaned an important 'legacy' from Argyle from which every Scottie lover can profit and grow.

A wise teacher once told me, "... *when you come to the end of your life, the only question that will matter is: did I love well?*" This truth goes beyond our Scotties, of course, to touch the core of the meaning of life itself. But this truth about loving well certainly includes our Scotties along with everyone else in our circles of companionship. The legacy of Argyle teaches at least five key components of truly loving well.

Today Is Our Only Tomorrow

'Tomorrow' is the enemy of today. It is so easy to substitute intentions for actions in our relationships. 'Getting around to it' proves elusive. The fallacy in our assumptions, of course, is that we actually have tomorrows. Truth is, the only tomorrow any of us have for sure is today. The Buckinghams learned that truth because of Argy's terminal condition, but each of us, and each of our Scotties, has no guaranteed tomorrows, either. Argyle's legacy is clear: if you are going to love well, do not wait; do it today!

No Regrets

It was Stephen who said in our interview, "... *just be sure you live so there are no regrets. Don't leave things undone. Love each day so there are no regrets.*" Jewish teachers used to say, there is coming a Day when God will hold each person accountable for the good in life they failed to enjoy. I have always thought that made a lot of sense. As I get older it is clear to me it is not the mistakes I regret; it is the things I did not try! Argyle's gift to us is the great truth: do it!

Count Your Blessings

Taking loved ones for granted is almost a working definition of family! And often we obsess about what we lack to the point we forget to be truly grateful for what we have. There is an old gospel song, the refrain of which says, "... *Count your blessings, name them one by one.*" It is amazing how the palpable presence of death re-prioritizes life. When the illusion of tomorrow vanishes, the gift of today takes on a whole new meaning! Argyle's legacy to us is: do not take blessings for granted; treasure each one.

Power of Little Things

When it comes down to it, it is not big events but little things that give our souls texture. We can waste a lot of opportunities to make little memories while waiting for the big event that perhaps never comes. Our Scotties need little to be transported into ecstacy. Argy loved his 'boomer ball.' Merely the tinkle of a collar and leash sent him into spasms of delight. A walk. A silent pat and rub. A ride in the car. Little things. Argyle reminds us there is power in little things, and that power is available to each of us.

Life Is For Living

Perhaps the most important aspect of Argyle's legacy is the lesson that death is about life! What I mean is that for the Buckinghams the knowledge of terminal illness was not a signal to draw the shades and quit. Instead, it was a wake-up call to live! Argyle refused to die till it was time. To the very end, through the chemotherapy and radical treatments, he chased life with true Scottie vigor and gusto. For the Buckinghams life was full because death gave them a sense of urgency to live fully. Truth is, we're all terminal. The only difference is our illusions. Diagnosis stripped illusions away for the Buckinghams and their experience of loving well is richer for it.

Conclusion

So there they are, lessons on loving well, a legacy from a very special Scottie who, as Scripture says, "... *being dead, yet speaketh.*" From Argyle and the Buckingham's 15-month ordeal with death and dying we can learn important truths about loving well for our own Scottie companionship, and, indeed, for our lives as a whole. Argyle's legacy to us is that today is our only tomorrow, that we should pursue love without regrets, and count our blessings, and cherish the power of little things, and, above all, to know that as long as there is life, it is for living.

Argyle died the morning of June 3rd, 1996, after a hard fight against his cancer. Throughout the 15-months of treatment Liz made it a point to regularly tell Argy, *"You're my little gentleman."*

In his legacy of loving well bequeathed to Scottie lovers everywhere Argyle is revealed to be in the best British sense, *both* "a gentleman and a scholar!"

Following private cremation Argy was buried near his Garden Fairy in his favorite spot in his yard. Photo by Stephen Buckingham.

Further Reading

This chapter first appeared as *"On Loving Well: Legacy of Argyle Hopscotch Buckingham,"* by Joseph Harvill, in ***GSM***, Vol 1 No 4 (Jul/Aug) 1996. Today the Buckinghams have a new Scottie, Aviemore, from Nova Scotia.

CHAPTER FIFTEEN

Rewards:
Inside the Pay-offs of Scottie Love

Ask the residents of Jerrell, Texas, and they will tell you in no uncertain terms. Their lives were mangled by a Force 5 tornado that blew away their world in an instant. Ask a young mother of two in Tennessee who is losing her battle against breast cancer. Or ask a 12 year-old boy in Tucumcari, New Mexico, whose attorney father committed suicide and whose mother and two sisters died two months later in a road accident. Ask them and they will tell you life can be brutal. It is not melodrama but experience which teaches us that life can hurt a lot.

No wonder, then, that we seek security wherever we can find it— in religion, in physical fitness, in self-help courses and therapy. But the impersonal character of our world penetrates our defenses. We struggle to make sense of the nonsense in our lives.

For Scottie lovers it is the unconditional love of our dogs which makes a harsh world bearable. Scotties are security blankets for us in a profound sense, about which I have written elsewhere (see: *"Why Do I Hurt So Much?"* chapter 22).

The remarkable experience of being chosen by a Scottie helps explain the success of the program known as Scottie Rescue. Scottie communion fosters deep stewardship toward the breed and this new stewardship generates meaning and focus for Scottie lovers all across the country.

Over the past ten years Scottie Rescue has gone from marginality to an honored place in the Scottish Terrier Club of America's agenda, and become a household word in the Scottie community. It is a regionally organized adoption program set up to rescue Scotties from animal control shelters and potential euthanasia, and to place them in suitable Scottie-lover homes.

Because of the importance of Scottie Rescue both to the dogs we love as well as to ourselves, it is worth probing beneath the surface to discern the hidden rewards at work in this great program. As an armchair anthropologist, and avid student of American culture, I believe there are deep and powerful 'pay-backs' in rescue work which off-set sacrifices and which bring workers back for more. Let me tease out four such rewards which I believe drive Scottie Rescue at its best, rewards that are not only profound pay-offs in the lives of volunteers but also compelling incentives for every reader to get involved.

Immediate Gratification

So much of modern life seems intractable. Despite our technological genius and drive for resolution and closure, ancient problems of starvation, poverty, disease, hatred, and violence defy human solution. The 20th century spawned two world wars "to end all wars." Yet today war looms closer to us than ever. More than innocent lives were lost in the terrorist bombing of Oklahoma City. Illusions of Mayberry, USA, died, too.

At the personal level, gender wars and political correctness fray relationships at home and in the workplace, and consumerism, with its siren voice of self-indulgence, alienates us from the self-discipline necessary to break lifestyle habits which threaten our survival. Resolution and closure elude us at all levels. Progress has the disturbing appearance of one step forward and two steps back.

By contrast, Scottie Rescue holds out the delicious opportunity for real resolution and closure on a problem of life and death proportions. In contrast to all that is intractable in modern life, before which the individual stands helpless and bewildered, saving a Scottie through Scottie Rescue is something the ordinary Scottie lover can do, and often with dramatic results! Those results are visible in the dogs who are hungry for love, and manifest in their adoptors, eager for a companion.

That is not to say that every Scottie rescue is a success made in heaven. But it is to say that, to those who have shared at any level in the bonding of rescued Scotties there is immediate gratification over solving a life-threatening problem. As editor of *Great Scots Magazine*, my files are full of ecstatic letters from Scottie Rescue owners whose lives are enriched beyond measure by the rescued dogs in their homes. And in the local cases of Scottie rescue in which I have had opportunity to observe first hand the Scotties themselves, I have seen clearly in the non-verbal but articulate body-language of the dogs the joy of renewed bonds of trust in humans.

It is not often in our world in matters of life and death importance that we get a shot at immediate gratification. But Scottie Rescue is just such an opportunity.

Savior Roles

Another of the deep incentives which fuels participation in Scottie Rescue is the opportunity close and small to play the part of a christ-figure whose acts redeem and save the lost.

Messiahship and the redemptive impulse are deeply embedded in our Judaeo-Christian culture. Those of us raised on Gospel hymns and biblical stories know that redemption and atonement are not only part of our everyday language (e.g., "scape-goat," an Old Testament redemption-figure which carried away the peoples' sins, "Judas," as contemporary synonym for traitor, etc.), but the duty to save and redeem is in our culture's bones. Why else do

Scottie Rescue 'Foster Parents, Ken Hutchison and Tonya Morrow, Lafayette, CO., share affection with 8 yr old rescue Scottie, 'Mr. McGoo.' Loving, competent foster homes are the greatest need in rescue programs everywhere.

we provide free shelter, food, clothing, education, healthcare, job training, and legal access to frivolous litigation to incarcerated social pariahs, while we chase innocent homeless, who receive no entitlements, out of city parks? Our cultural drive to redeem may be misguided, but there is no doubt the messiah-complex is a real and potent force in our society.

But so often in modern experience our redemptive acts backfire and seem more a menace than a help. Whether one looks at our penal system or our foreign aid programs our savior roles appear to garner more resentment and hatred than gratitude. At the individual level our culture is so schizophrenic that good Samaritans are as likely to be sued as to be thanked!

But rescuing Scotties is a welcome difference. Mark Twain said, "If you pick up a starving dog and make him prosperous, he will not bite you. That is the principal difference between a dog and a man." And that is the principal difference between redemptive programs aimed at innocent animals and those aimed at humans. People, it seems, have lost the gift of being thankful. Entitlements have made us rude and shrill and irascible. They have also taken much

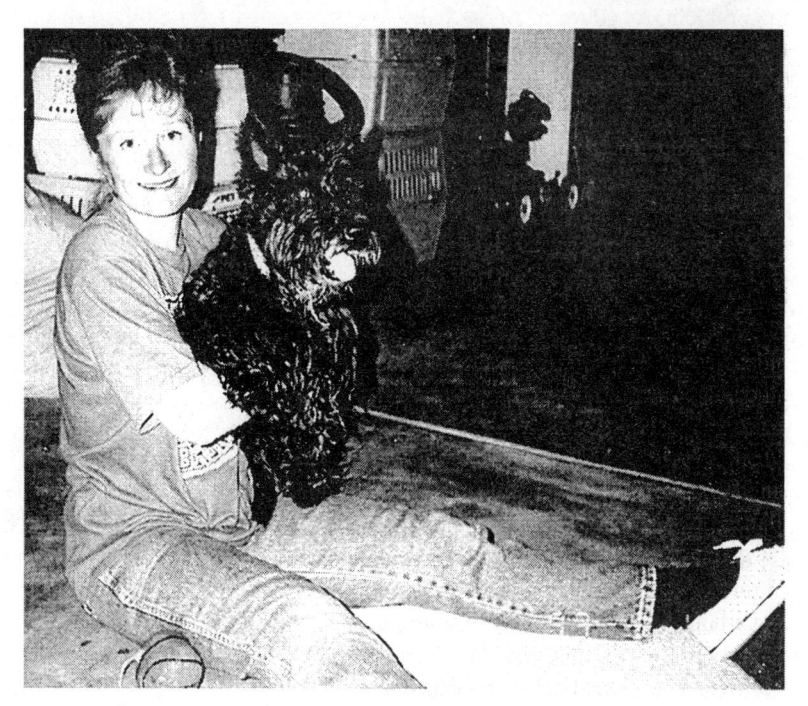

Sally Gilman, Co-Director of the Rocky Mountain Scottish Terrier Club Rescue Program, Arvada, CO., one of the oldest organized programs in the country, takes time to 'give back' to one of her "rescue fur-kids." Photo: Don Gilman.

A second-hand Scottie makes a first-rate pet. One of the Rocky Mountain Scottish Terrier Club's rescue dogs makes a new friend. Photo by Don Gilman

of the joy from acts of kindness.

Not so with Scotties. Unlike people, they have loyalty and companionship embedded in their DNA. They can express more authentic thanksgiving with their tail in minutes than a human can express with their tongue in hours. Again and again in adoption-placement situations I have seen Scotties with bad reputations seemingly go out of their way to say thank you and to fit into the welcome of their benefactors. I also have seen that special Scottie thank you change the lives of their saviors. Bill Barnes, of Tijeras, New Mexico, who opened his heart and home to a rescued Scottie from Idaho, is today a changed man according to his wife. 'Andy' and Bill are inseparable today and Bill will be the first to tell you that to save a Scottie is to redeem most of all your own best self.

Giving Back

I believe the third of the deeper reasons why Scottie Rescue workers discover such rare satisfaction in their work is the sheer pleasure of giving back to the breed that has given them so much.

It was Jesus who taught that there is more happiness in giving than in receiving, and that when you give generously, it comes back to you, "... *good measure, pressed down, shaken together, and running over, shall men give into your bossom.*" Truer words were never spoken than these when applied to

Second-hand Scotties need a second-chance at love, and bereft Scottie lovers need a deserving Scottie to spoil. Scottie Rescue is often the perfect match. Photo by D.Gilman.

the 'return' experienced by those who give themselves in the service of Scottie Rescue.

And as Jesus' words imply, and the best of human experience confirms, giving which is from the heart turns into getting and getting received with grace turns into giving in a profound and wonderful reflexivity which defies logic. Scottie rescuers know that logic; they know the ineffable bounty which comes of giving with their hearts.

Giving from the heart, however, is not easy, not merely because our cynical era has prostituted pathos and sentiment rendering all talk of heartfelt matters suspect, but because to give from one's heart is to be attached, it is to care, it is to expose oneself to emotional hurt and pain. At the same time it is also to know authentic love and joy. The truth is, both loss and love are the legacies of true giving.

To know Rescue Scotties, and to love them, not as furniture, but as companions on your journey of life is to know what strained and anxious lives they have led. It is to share the pain of their abandonment, to share in some sense the trauma of being emotionally unrequited in the world of Persons, whose affections they have sought endlessly to secure, whose authority they were expected unquestioningly to obey, and whose loyalty and trust, for whatever reasons, they now have lost. Their burden is a bewilderment and hurt which they cannot possibly comprehend. But to love such a Scottie with the soft hands and heart of the true giver is to give back fidelity and loyalty worthy of the great gifts in kind which the dogs routinely give, "... *pressed down, shaken together, and running over*," to all whom they know and love.

Purpose

The fourth of the deeper reasons why Scottie Rescue brings rich rewards is the sense of purpose it brings to one's life.

Now this need for meaning in life, for a sense that we are part of a purpose bigger and more significant than ourselves, that somehow we will leave a mark and that our life will have made a difference, is at the center of what it means to be human. I believe we are most alive when we are devoted to a cause large enough to be worthy of our soul.

But finding such a worthy cause in our cynical age is not easy. Past generations found identity and meaning in the church or other social institutions as centers of faith and progress. However, sexual scandal and revelations of corruption at highest levels of both sacred and secular institutions leave thoughtful moderns convinced bureaucracies of all types are part of our problem, not the solution. Furthermore, it is easy for today's 'causes' to appear global and overwhelming and impervious to the individual. Globalization of markets, technology, and popular culture has shriveled our sense we can individually make any difference.

And this is our modern predicament: our culture has globalized the surface of our lives while leaving the basic issues of human *Being* unaddressed.

However, the basic human quest for meaning does not go away, it merely goes underground. By day we work with statistics; in the evenng we consult astrologers and frighten ourselves with thrillers about vampires. The abyss between the rational and the spiritual, the external and the internal, the objective and the subjective, the technical and the moral, the universal and the unique daily grows deeper.

And that is where Scottie Rescue comes in. For here is a cause which gives lives meaning and purpose— meaning in an ultimate, life and death sense— and at the same time is a cause

*"I am very little small mis'able dog . . . .
I do not understand."*
Illustration by G.L. Stampa, from
Rudyard Kipling, **Thy Servant A Dog**.
London: Macmillan, 1930.

susceptible to individual intervention. In this program an individual's concrete volunteer action makes a difference, a difference in the life of an innocent animal, and a difference in the life of a fortunate Scottie lover.

Such meaning and purpose in one's life is not trivial. To know that your action saved a life and fostered happiness and companionship is to know a deep satisfaction in your soul. As Sally Gilman, Co-Director of The Rocky Mountain Scottie Rescue puts it:

"I used to wonder what my purpose was in life, but not any more. When I share the grief of those who've lost their Scotties and then share the joys of placing a rescue Scottie in those homes, I know why I was spared in that terrible auto crash years ago that took the life of my sister. I have a purpose, a mission, a work to do. I've found that purpose in Scottie Rescue."

Rescue owner, Terry Olson, Aurora, CO., gets a kiss from 'Shadow,' his 4-5 yr old rescue Scottie. Photo by Sally Gilman.

Conclusion

It is true life can be brutal. Life can also bring very great rewards.

It is because we know how brutal life can be that we reach out in compassion to innocent animals brutalized by circumstance. And in the rescuing, it is the rescuers who are most profoundly blessed. In practice, Scottie Rescue becomes an organized way for those who have been touched by Scottie-love to honor the debt owed to this special breed.

The remarkable rewards we receive by participating in Scottie Rescue, rewards of immediate gratification, opportunity to fill a savior role, the gift of giving back to the dogs who have given us so much, and the blessing of a sense of purpose in our lives— these rewards are not the ultimate motivation for getting involved. These are rationalizations. The real motivation lies deeper. It is the heart, not the head, which is the ultimate driving force of Scottie Rescue. To connect with these dogs in their need, is to act from the heart.

The heart-response to which I refer is illustrated by a wealthy Scrooge-figure in a large city, a man of money and power, a man who had everything in his life except love and affection. He was on his way to a dinner in his honor at which business associates were to recognize his achievements as a captain of industry. On a street corner he passed a homeless boy who was staring at toys in a store window, and there was something about the sorrow in the young kid's eyes that made the man pause instead of rushing past as was his practice. The grief of life itself was distilled in that haunted young face and it stopped the man dead in his tracks. On impulse, listening for once to his heart rather than his head, he pulled money from his pocket, took the waif by the shoulder, and went into the store to buy the kid his impossible dream.

The poor boy was dumbfounded. As the rich man turned to walk away, embarrassed by his own impulsive generosity, the boy said to him, "Mister, if I had a Dad, I'd want him to be just like you!"

The man never made it to his business dinner. Hours later, when he finally showed up weary and exhausted, anxious friends asked what had happened. He told them about meeting the boy and his impulse gift, and about what the boy said to him in thanks.

"But that was hours ago," they protested.

"But you don't understand," he replied. "I've been driving around town looking for another little boy to help."

And that is precisely what fuels the rescue programs across the country. The Scotties that are rescued, in their own articulate ways, say eloquently, *"If I had a Master, I would want her to be just like you."*

Having known that unforgettable Scottie response we find ourselves searching everywhere for another wee Scottie to help.

Further Reading

This chapter first appeared under the same title in *GSM*, Vol 2 No 5 (Sep/Oct) 1997.

For information on Scottie Rescue, the program and how you may get involved, contact Daphne Branzell, national chairperson, at 5810 Windvale Dr., Windcrest, TX 78239. Phone: 210/ 653-3723, E-mail: scotswind@aol.com; or Sally Gilman, 7528 Queen Circle, Arvada, CO., 80005. Phone: 303/420-5071, E-mail: mackrail@uswest.net.

Part Three:
Celebrating the Scottie Good Life

Recounting the Sunshine

"The average dog is a nicer person than the average person."

Andrew A. Rooney

CHAPTER SIXTEEN

McKnight & A Damsel In Distress

An alarm went off somewhere deep in my soul. Something was wrong. Visions of dog-knappers selling stolen pets to research labs flashed through my mind, mingled with images of a helpless, lost puppy, too new to us to know how to find her way back home again. I stood still as death looking into the backyard as fireworks of anger, despair, and panic burst in my head.

I started calling her name wildly, "Nati! Nati! Come here girl. Dad's home!," trying to mask my panic. I called again, and again. No response. I raced into the backyard, checked behind the garage, quickly surveyed the new fence noting each place I earlier identified as vulnerable and carefully rebuilt.

Nothing. No signs of digging; no evidence of foul-play. No Scottie pup.

Despite everything I had done to secure our backyard encompassing two weeks of tough posthole digging and new fence building preceeded by weeks of meticulous planning and preparation so nothing was left to chance, nothing overlooked that could spoil our new beginnings; despite everything, our new Scottie puppy was nowhere to be found. The spunky pup that had so quickly and thoroughly stolen our hearts was gone, leaving me an ache from a Scottie-shaped hole at the center of me!

I jumped into the car and began canvassing our neighborhood, terrified at each turn I'd find my heart in the street somewhere in a crushed Scottie-fur coat.

I called. I whistled. I called some more.

Criss-crossing our sub-division, I drove for blocks in all directions asking everyone in sight if they'd seen a Scottie pup wearing a tartan collar.

Nothing. No clues. No Nati.

Then the storm came. Snowflakes the size of Texas fell that February afternoon as I raced around the neighborhood searching every nook and cranny.

As darkness fell the temperature dropped like a brick, bringing the worst ice storm Kentucky had seen in years. Whole trees snapped. Power lines were down. Neighborhoods were without electricity. If our missing pup somehow survived the busy streets, we knew the freezing temperatures would kill her for sure.

We were so depressed that night we could do little more than take turns crying on each other's shoulder.

To some folks it may appear excessive for two educated adults to suffer the anguish and pain we felt that night over a dog—and a new dog of less than two weeks, at that! I know to that half of the population who are not dog lovers such trauma over a new puppy is mindless blubbering.

My reply is that Life has taught me such heart matters, laden with sentiment, are the pieces of our days most worth remembering.

Whether the non-dog crowd can understand that or not, I know I cried my eyes out over a lost dog that awful winter night.

I cannot adequately explain why Nati's loss was so painful to me at that early point in our life together, anymore than I can adequately explain why there are two kinds of people, those who love dogs and those who don't. But I can attest that the pain was acute.

I can rationalize an answer: she was a love child of sorts, an anniversary gift to ourselves on our fourth wedding anniversary; true, too, it was love at first sight, our special communion began at the outset when she went to sleep in my arms after a tummy rub on the very first trip home from Cincinnati; and my sweat equity in that little dog was considerable since I had invested days that were in scarce supply at that time rebuilding our backyard fence to make our yard secure.

But I am the first to say that each of these or all of them together cannot rationally add up to the grieving I felt. I was shattered. A mere two week's time?— that is true. A mere dog?— not exactly.

Looking back now on that crisis I believe I knew from the very first there was a knitting of hearts between us, a super glue instant bond that was somehow a gift from a higher source. Scottie lovers will understand, something at the center of me was missing, and I was in great pain. Simply put, I loved that little Scottie and I had lost my love.

I have thought a lot about the pain of loving and about the heart's reasons that appear so irrational to the head. The truth is, in matters of the heart time is no measure. That is because bonding is a matter of the soul, not of the clock, and when spirits touch "one day is as a thousand years, and a thousand years a day." In less time than it takes to form a new habit she touched me forever.

That is my take on it at least. I hurt so much that night because I already loved her more than I could say. And the thought of her being lost, or hurt, or dead made that freezing February night the longest ever in the Bluegrass.

Next morning we distributed flyers in the neighborhood, put an ad in the Lexington newspaper, and ran an ad on local radio. We did everything we could think of to alert the world to our missing Scottie pup wearing a tartan collar.

Hopes were high at first. Everytime the phone rang we leaped with anticipation.

Nothing.

By the end of the first week we were in the pit of despair, again. The second week we languished to new depths of hopelessness when nothing turned up.

But the Great Scottie in the sky moves in mysterious ways her wonders to perform! Unknown to us in our grief a McKnight in his own kind of shining armor had come to our rescue.

The McKnights lived about two miles from us, across busy intersections and traffic arteries. Mr. McKnight was out gathering fire wood in the snow storm when he found a wet, shivering Scottie puppy near exhaustion, wearing a tartan collar. He took her in, fed her warm milk, and Mrs. McKnight made her a cozy bed in a laundry basket near their gas heater.

That could have been the end of the story—a puppy found and adopted, the original owners never knowing what happened to their beloved dog lost in a snow storm. But the story does not end there because some very real Scottie magic was at work in this case.

The McKnights did not know us and had no idea we had lost our new Scottie. They were retirees who did not keep up with newspapers or the radio and had no idea of our frantic search. None of their close neighbors knew anything about the little Scottie, either. All the McKnights knew about the little dog was she showed up half dead wearing a tartan collar.

Two miles away, however, at our house, the longest two weeks on record passed by. With each day our hope died.

"If someone found her," I remember lamenting to Charlotte, "and if they were going to return her, they would have called by now. One way or another, she's gone for good."

But Scottie fortune smiled through a string of events almost too good to be true. Although the McKnights missed our ads, someone on the other side of town had seen our lost dog ad and proved the link in this drama.

Mr. McKnight's neighbor, who knew he found a stray Scottie pup, *happened* to visit an elderly friend on the other side of Lexington, and in making conversation *happened* to mention the Scottie stray with the tartan collar that showed up at her neighbor's house during the snow storm. Well, it *so happened* that the elderly friend on the other side of town, while bundling up newspapers for recycling, *happened* to notice a two-week old ad about a missing Scottie puppy wearing a tartan collar. Mr. McKnight's neighbor salvaged the ad with our phone number and took it back to Mr. McKnight.

I can still remember the disbelief in my voice when I answered the phone and Mr. McKnight told me he had our Nati. I was afraid to believe him, but afraid not to. I could not risk getting my hopes up again.

He must have heard the pain in my voice because he proceeded to reassure me by saying all the right things. He told me the story of the rescue in the snow storm, of wrapping the little waif in towels to warm her chilled body, of the laundry basket bed near the furnace, and of his growing affection for her.

He came straight over to our house that night. I can remember as if it were yesterday the anxiety I felt waiting for the doorbell to ring. It seemed to take hours for them to travel the two miles to our house.

When we opened our front door, there she was with her impish face staring out at us from inside Mr. McKnight's overcoat.

Instantly our world was right again!

That night Mr. McKnight came carrying Nati back into our lives, and she *happened* to be wearing her tartan collar, and he brought his friend who *happened* to talk to a friend across town who *happened* to read the ad about a lost Scottie in a tartan collar.

Happenstance? Coincidence? Luck?

Maybe.

I prefer to believe the Scottie angels smiled on me. As I reflect on that crisis and its unlikely resolution, I do not put much stock in luck. Not if by luck you mean random coincidence. I believe there is meaning in events even when we ourselves cannot find it. Things do not just happen. There is purpose, meaning, and inter-connection in all things, including Scotties.

It was the day after Nati returned to us, almost by accident, I discovered the secret of her escape from our yard that dreadful day. I was building a

cabinet in my garage shop and had spread out onto the driveway. Knowing I could not watch her every minute and being unwilling to risk another episode of wandering, I put Nati in the backyard and closed the high gate. Now that heavy wooden gate turned out to be our vulnerable spot. Before Nati came home to us from Cincinnati I rebuilt our backyard fence with new posts and small mesh wire making our fence impossible to get through; the high fence had to be climbed. But climbing seemed an unfair penalty to Chessie, our housecat. So I cut a small rounded hole at ground level in the heavy gate beside the house.

I cut the hole small for a slender, small-sized cat, and even she had to flatten herself to squeeze through it. "Far too small an opening for a six month old Scottie with a large head!," I reassured myself.

She showed me never to underestimate her again. As I sanded the cabinet frame in our driveway I saw first her large nose in the almost mouse-size hole at the bottom of the gate, then her muzzle; then her eyebrows and flattened ears poked through, and almost magically, her whole frolicking puppy body popped out of that hole quick as a flash like a newborn expelled in birthing!

I could not believe she could worm through that tiny hole. But then Nati taught me to believe many things I thought impossible. Chessie lost her 'door' in the gate after that and I learned an important truth about the kingdom of heaven: a 'camel' *can* pass through the eye of a needle!

The unlikelihood of Nati's escape from our yard, of her survival, and of her return; the unlikelihood of the thread of events which brought her back to us, leave me more than ever inclined to believe in guardian angels.

And something else. That unlikely rescue and return taught me to love Don Quixote in a new and wonderful sense, to believe in modern chivalry and knights in shining armor. At least, that night through the strange and wonderful interposings of unlikely events Nati taught me to celebrate the magic of the impossible dream.

These days whenever I look at her photo or remember the countless quiet times we shared over our years together I know I have my own chivalrous 'knight' to thank for my memories. And I say a quiet little prayer of thanks to the guardian angels wherever they are who sent to the Bluegrass a 'McKnight in shining armor' to save our little damsel in distress.

A Scottie much-loved never dies,
Since being apart magnifies
the joys that were shared,
the dreams that were dared—
and the hole at the center her size.
©1999 Joseph Harvill

---

*This chapter is a revised version of the first story ever published in *Great Scots Magazine*. It appeared as *"McKnight and the Damsel in Distress,"* by Joseph Harvill, *GSM*, Vol 1 No 1 (Jan/Feb) 1996.

'Miss Nati,' the little Scottie dog who inspired *Great Scots Magazine*, died at age 12 craddled in the author's arms on a cold February day in 1999. Her sweet spirit and quiet dignity are celebrated by all who knew her.

In Praise of Imperfection

"A Scottie shaved!" she said aghast,
scarcely hiding wonderment.
Then turned to speak of class and form
and proper Scottie temperament.

'Proper,' indeed, I thought to myself
to whom? to what? and why?
Could I love her more in another's skin?
Would ribbons change my eye?

My mind slipped back to countless baths,
to vets and pills and lotions;
to near-death times and quiet times,
to scrapbook of emotions.

"She has bad skin," I heard me say;
but that's not the story's end.
She's more than a champ to me, you see,
she's family, pal, and Friend!

Joseph Harvill
For Nati
©1998

CHAPTER SEVENTEEN

Bird Dog with a Brogue

Lee Netzler

We arrived at the parking area 30 minutes before the legal hunting start time. I counted 14 vehicles already parked, and at least twice that many hunters with their dogs nervously ambling about. And they were BIG dogs— Labradors, English Springers, Brittanys, and German Shorthairs. By comparison, my little Scottish Terrier, Rusty, looked like an out-of-place child's toy. We were surrounded on all sides by confident, heavily-equipped, big-time hunters and their huge, muscular, experienced bird dogs.

My confidence withered. I was totally intimidated. But seeing Rusty's eagerness, I somehow hung on to my determination that, no matter what, my bird dog with a brogue was going to go out and hunt with the best of them!

I got my gear ready and collected my courage waiting as long as I could before getting Rusty out of the Jeep, trying to avoid the scrutiny and hard looks I knew we would get. Finally, with 15 minutes to go, I hooked the bright blaze-orange lead to his bell collar, took a deep breath, and stepped into the parking lot.

There was an immediate hush among the hunters, followed by harsh whispers as we crossed the lot and set out for the hunting area. "No matter what they think," I said to Rusty, "we're here to stay!" Little did I know what my bird dog with a brogue had in store for his partner that day.

My adventure with Scotties as bird dogs started several years ago when my previous Scottie, Piper, accidentally flushed a big rooster pheasant and the rush of that excitement left him and me forever eager to track any fresh pheasant scent. Over the years Piper and I shared many special hours together in the field bird hunting. My fond memories of those adventures with Piper led me to try to teach my young Scottie, Rusty, who is 1 1/2 years old, to track pheasants.

I placed a telephone order with a hunting supply company and in a few days their package arrived at our door. It contained a large canvas dumbbell, a 4 ounce bottle of liquid pheasant training scent, and thin brochure which outlined how to use the materials to train a bird dog. I quickly discovered that the large dumbbell, while suitable for an adult pointer or retriever, was much too big for my 20 pound Scottie. And the booklet wasn't much help, either. We postponed the start of our training and reordered a 'puppy' sized dumbbell.

When the replacement order arrived I started by putting Rusty on a 'sit-stay' in the living room. After smearing a little of the pheasant-scented liquid on the canvas dumbbell I tied it to a string and dragged it across the room. Then, with great enthusiasm I shouted, "*Find the bird!*" He shot across the room in a blur to investigate the marvelous new object. As he ran, I voiced my encouragement loudly, and when he found it, I rewarded him with a stream of praise and a small treat. After a few more 'finds,' he was hooked! It was a wonderful game full of suspense, excitement, lavish praise and best of all, topped off by a tasty treat every time he responded to "Find the bird!"

We repeated these exercises almost daily, as I dragged the dumbbell a little further away from him each time we practiced. When he proved he could "Find the bird" anywhere in the house, we graduated to the yard. I began to leave him inside the house while I went outside to lay the track. I would bring him outside to the starting point and cheer him on as he unerringly followed his nose to the hidden dumbbell.

Next we graduated to the local parks. I laid scent trails through tall grasses and over rougher terrain and gradually lengthened the distance. Rusty improved to the point he could consistently track the dumbbell through 50 or 60 yards of rough cover. As he successfully handled each new challenge my appreciation of his ability grew. Of course, he always got plenty of praise and a small treat when he accomplished the 'find.'

In September Rusty went along on a three week traveling vacation.

We played "Find the bird!" at campgrounds in Kansas, Missouri, Arkansas, Oklahoma, New Mexico, and Colorado. Despite the unfamiliar settings he almost always earned his treat. My confidence was growing that he might soon be ready to go after the real thing.

After our vacation I took Rusty hiking a few times in the mountains near our home in Longmont, Colorado. It is an area where upland game birds are occasionally found and I wanted to expose him to the scent of the real thing. These hikes did not directly improve his pheasant skills, but I learned a great deal about reading his body language and his vocal signals as he demonstrated ability to distinguish fresh deer trails and to track ground squirrels. I knew he had real scent abilities. But was he ready for an actual pheasant hunt?

Clad in their brightly-colored safety hunting vests, Lee Netzler and Scottish Terrier hunting companion, Rusty, share a day together in the field hunting game birds. Photo by Lee Netzler.

In late October it was time for my annual pheasant hunting trip to my brother-in-law's in Wisconsin. Don and his veteran Brittany Spaniel, Bingo, are serious, no-nonsense pheasant hunters, so the prospect of a would-be bird dog with a brogue tagging along gave me serious pause. I believed in his ability, however, so I decided it was time to sink or swim. He was coming with me to Wisconsin!

I did not let Rusty go with Don and me on the hunts over the span of Don's vacation. Don's dog, Bingo, showed her magic and we brought home many pheasants. Rusty carefully examined all the birds we brought home, and seemed to say to me after inspecting each lot, *"OK. When is it MY turn?"*

My plan was to give my Scottie his hunting debut after my brother-in-law's vacation ended and he returned to work. I still wondered whether we were ready for the big time so on Monday morning Rusty and I drove to the 4,500 acre Bong State Recreation Area in southeastern Wisconsin to look things over together. I intentionally timed our trip so that we arrived well after most of the hunters were already gone for the day to minimize the confusion and disruption I feared other hunters and dogs would cause us. Once there Rusty worked the cover, explored the scents, and heard his first sounds of nearby gunfire. I was very pleased with how well he handled his initiation experience he was well behaved and poised, very attentive to the bird signs all around us. I knew then we were ready.

So there we sat the following morning surrounded by veteran pheasant hunters and their incredibly athletic bird dogs, waiting for the start time to enter the field. I felt like David against Goliath. Would we be the laughing stock of everyone present that day? I could imagine the sneers about my bird dog without legs! I took a deep breath and opened the door. Rusty was going to have his chance! Ignoring the hard looks and chortles, we headed for the field.

It was very cold as we walked into a stiff wind. Hard for the shooter, I thought, but good for the dog. As we headed into the wind and down a long narrow strip of field created by two loose boundaries on either side, I rubbed my watering eyes and chanted, *"Find the Bird!, Rusty."*

He worked eagerly, left and right, keeping abreast or slightly ahead of me.

Fifty yards ahead a white speck caught my eye and I rubbed my eyes and squinted to make out what it was. I could not believe what I saw! The white spot was the ring on a rooster's neck. Suddenly *two* roosters shuffled nervously at our approach. My mind raced furiously, trying to develop a plan as we continued to close on them. I knew the birds would probably run, and that only strong pressure would force them into the air for a shot. Oh, what to do next?!

Then, at 25 yards, the two roosters ducked their heads and ran. I took up the chase, running as fast as I could, with a bewildered Rusty struggling along behind, trying to keep up. The two birds split, and I raced after the one angling off to the right. I soon lost sight of my quary but kept running hard after it, following the direction it was heading. After another 25 steps it suddenly flushed 25 yards in front of me. I stopped, braced, fired, and then fired again. On the second shot the rooster tumbled down about 50 yards away.

Any experienced pheasant hunter will testify that a downed pheasant is the most elusive thing on earth! I grimmaced and threw down my cap to mark the spot where I thought the bird landed. I immediately began searching, but I knew my chances were bad and getting worse with each passing second.

As I bumbled back and forth looking for the wounded bird in the thick grass and weeds, Rusty finally caught up with me. I quickly showed Rusty the place marked by my cap and half-heartedly urged him to "Find the Bird!"

To my surprise Rusty picked up the scent at the spot and began tracking the bird for 15 yards to where the pheasant was hiding. I heard the exploding of wings as Rusty flushed the bird and turned to see him bounding along almost directly under the rising rooster! This time my shot was accurate. A moment later we tucked one handsome rooster into our game pouch.

I was so proud of Rusty! I am convinced we would never have gotten that bird if Rusty had not tracked it down and flushed it the second time. The nearest hunter to our position, who witnessed the whole episode, paused briefly as he passed by to ask, *"What kind of dog is that?"* When I replied, *"A Scottish Terrier,"* he did not seem to believe me. But as he walked away he shrugged and left us with the compliment that he did not think anybody could do much better than we had just done.

Lee Netzler and his 'bird dog with a brogue' with their trophies from a successful pheasant hunt in Wisconsin. Rusty the Scottish Terrier out performed the canine 'pros.' Photo by Lee Netzler.

But my bird dog with a brogue was not finished showing us his stuff. After his rightful praise and a treat, we got reorganized, and set off again. After just a few minutes, Rusty picked up a really hot scent. He pressed hard following the track and I had to hurry to keep up with him. I kept peering ahead, hoping to catch a glimpse of whatever it was we were chasing. Suddenly, there it was. I was stunned to see a rooster and two hens on the run only 40 yards in front of us! Then a third hen emerged and caught up with the others. A few seconds later, they all disappeared into the thick cover ahead of us.

I took off at a dead run, rushing after them in an attempt to flush them into the air. After sprinting 40 or 50 yards, the rooster and two hens flew up well ahead of me. I shot twice and the rooster dropped without moving.

What a day! I could not believe all that had happened. In just 25 minutes Rusty and I had our legal limit of two fine rooster pheasants. I caught my breath, gave Rusty his treat and a drink of water, unloaded the shotgun, and started planning our victory walk back to the parking lot! I carefully positioned the birds in my game pouch to gaudily display gorgeous rooster tails sticking out of BOTH sides for all to see. I kept a few steps behind Rusty all the way back to the parking lot, and flashed a Chesshire Cat smile each time we passed one of the other hunters. Rusty and I were so proud of ourselves I believe we could have walked on water!

Back at the parking lot, we were the only ones there everyone else was still in the field trying to fill their limit. Out of all the hunters with their classy bird dogs, Rusty and I were the first to get our limit that morning!

What a feeling! I was still shaking from the experience when we got back home and I haven't fully calmed down yet. Even now, I can relive the thrill of that day in my mind with perfect clarity.

What a triumph for Rusty! What a day together! It was one small step for a pheasant hunter; one giant leap for a bird dog with a brogue!

The author and his companion Scottie, Rusty, at their home in Longmont, CO. Photo by Lee Netzler.

*Reprinted from *GSM*, Vol 1 No 2 (Mar/Apr 1996).

CHAPTER EIGHTEEN

Only A Bump In The Road: Jet, the Paraplegic Scottie

Nicholas Nash

When I inherited my mother's paraplegic Scottish Terrier I wondered about my promise made to her that whenever the time came that she could not care for him, I would. 'Jet Lag,' as she called him, did not like men, strangers, people who delivered things, other dogs, and quick-footed small children. He did like women and dinner, especially dinner. Beyond these defects of character, his back legs did not work. If they had worked his aggressiveness might have forced him to an early end.

When Jet arrived in my mother's life he was a typical Scottie, although a bit more aggressive than most. Eventually, there was a spinal problem and his back legs became paralyzed at about the same time mother's health began to decline.

Jet's behavior worsened. Anyone within lunging distance was a target for a bite. It was not a good situation, but mother's rapidly failing health made it difficult for her to do much about it.

I came upon Jet shortly after mother died. He was in the hall, alone, and shaking. I am convinced he knew what had happened.

I picked him up and held him until he calmed down, and that began a

"Jet is the least handicapped animal I know," says owner Nicholas Nash of his ten year old paraplegic Scottish Terrier. Jet is shown here in his cumberbund ensconsed on his favorite bed. Photo by Nicholas Nash

relationship that has affected my life far more than I ever thought possible. The message from the veterinarian who had taken care of Jet was quite clear: Jet would only get worse so he should be put down. I told the vet we already had one death in the family that week and there would not be another.

So, we came back to Minnesota in the midst of winter, and our adventure together began. The Veterinary Teaching Hospital in St. Paul said Jet would not get better, but also that his paralysis would not likely get worse. For me that was good news.

I remember the first month as the month my back began to strengthen. Picking up Jet and putting him down what seemed to be 30 times a day served as an excellent exercise program. Jet's weight ranges between 24 to 27 pounds, but if he were a Saint Bernard my choices would have been more difficult! Because of our continual lifting routine Jet and I have formed a physical bond that is uncommon with Scotties, and now, after three years together, I do not even think about the exertion of lifting him anymore.

With the aid of his 'K-9 Cart' Jet pulls himself around the house without much difficulty and no complaint. With practice we have learned to utilize a towel-sling for outside walks, by which I support Jet's hindquarters at the proper height and he walks on his front legs.

Make no mistake about it, Jet is all Scottie! One warm, spring morning when we were doing extensive remodeling to our house, I went upstairs, leaving Jet safely, I thought, in the kitchen. When I returned the door to the deck had blown open and Jet was gone. I searched inside and out, but found no sign of him.

Panicked, I searched again in widening circles around the yard and finally, in the distance, noticed two ears sticking up just over the horizon at the edge of the lake. Jet had hauled himself through the kitchen and dinning room, across the deck, down the steps, across the lawn, and into the lake. There he sat in shallow water revelling in his adventure. That was the morning I learned it was important that Jet have opportunity to go on his own expeditions, within reason, and that I had to keep better track of his whereabouts.

As we became used to each other Jet's strength and confidence grew, and his improved muscle tone allowed him to get around more easily. The other two resident Scotties who owned me prior to Jet's coming into our home preferred to ignore Jet, but he would not let them. He liked to supervise dinner time and he would clean up the other two dogs' dinners, unless they growled him off. I thought the occasional growl-fest was a healthy sign as long as it did not turn into a real fight. Today, three years later, and despite his handicap, Jet's strong personality has made him 'alpha dog' among my three, his aggression has abated, and our lives together are generally harmonious.

As Jet's spirits rose he began to react like any other Scottie to the prospect of an adventure. He jumped up and down— on his front paws, at least— if a walk, ride, meal, or treat seemed near at hand. He also began to lie down and roll around on the carpet or grass, groaning with pleasure, something he never did before with his limited capacity for motion. Today, at age 10, Jet's favorite game is getting me on my back on the floor so he can roll onto my outstretched arms. He nuzzles me and even bestows an occasional lick— we have made progress!

The most frequently asked question I receive about Jet has to do with elimination or incontinence. All else pales before this challenge, but one's attitude has a lot to do with long-term success. Jet cannot feel anything below his mid-back, so figuring out his 'performance' schedule took a little time. Plastic baggies along with paper towels on every level of the house and a carpet-cleaning kit have been essential.

Other adjustments that have been made include adding vinyl flooring during recent remodeling, watching where we step, laundering cumberbunds and sanitary pads, and so on. Locating a knowledgeable, sympathetic vet who understands canine paraplegia has been crucial.

Medical care for a paraplegic Scottie is expensive since infections of the urinary tract are a constant problem and a 'maintenence dose' of anitbiotics is standard. Like any other unpleasant task, once dealing with it becomes part of your daily pattern, you do not think about it much. Really.

People frequently comment about my caregiving, about my difficulties and adjustments and what all I do for Jet. What they fail to see is what Jet does for me. When you live with a creature who does his best without complaint, who gets from place A to place B by pulling himself by his front paws and who does 360 degree spins under the same limitations, and who explores his environment with unbridled enthusiasm, greeting each day with a 'can-do!' spirit which seems to say, "Okay, life, what do you have for me today?"— and when you see this every single day, it has a profound impact. I get such positive energy from him and find rare joy in his successes. Jet is the least handicapped animal I know and I draw strength every day from his courage.

This little Scottie has changed me. I have learned something important from him about persistence, patience, and will. Dogs are not furniture to be disgarded when broken. I have learned paraplegia is not the end of the road for companions, it is only a bump in the road.

Jet is doing so well today. I only wish mother were here to see him thriving. There is no 'jet-lag' in Minnesota!

I confess I am grateful that Jet has only two good legs. He and I are better creatures for it. I am the blessed one in this relationship. His has been a wonderful gift, one which I can never fully repay.

Essential Ingredients for Living Well with a Paraplegic Scottie

Carts providing wheels for paraplegic dogs are very useful, but they do not solve every problem.

♦ A cumberbund with Velcro™ attachments and a beltless absorbent napkin is a problem-solver. Paraplegic dogs do well if they can spend a certain amount of time off the floor on an open-grid surface like Dri-Dek™ available through verinary supply catalogs.

♦ Pooch Pad,™ an absorbent sheet, can allow a dog into otherwise off-limits places and can prevent clean-ups if the cumberbund slips off, which is a regular occurrence.

♦ A diet that produces firm stools is essential.

♦ Disposable hospital pads are good for pets allowed on the bed.

♦ Prompt veterinary intervention is essential to treat skin and urinary tract infections that occur.

♦ Attitude is a key to success.

---

*This chapter is a revision of an article originally titled, "Not the End, Only A Bump In the Road," by Nicholas Nash, published in *GSM*, Vol 1 No 5 (Sep/Oct) 1996. Jet personified the epithet 'diehard' and was an inspiration to all who knew him. He passed away at his home in Minnesota in 1997 at age eleven.

CHAPTER NINETEEN

'June Bug' Therapy

Most folks do not like bugs. Spiders and creepy-crawlies give us the willies. And spot a cockroach or a termite and we are on the phone for help as if our clothes were on fire!

But in Bryn Mawr, Pennsylvania, there is a bug that no one fears and everyone delights to have around. That very special Pennsylvania 'bug' is a black Scottish Terrier named "June Bug" — "Buggie" for short— who is a trained therapy dog and a ministering angel to all who know her.

June Bug was born in June three years ago and now owns the Tunia Hyland family of Bryn Mawr— as well as the hearts of everyone else who has ever met her! Buggie is one of those rare and wonderful angels who loves everyone, and has the gift of making those with special needs feel valued and chosen. She is a smiler who, when greeting a friend new or old, throws her head back, curls her lip in a disarming smile, and then snorts and sneezes her own unforgettable Scottie version of a greeting something like, *"howdy-friend-how-in-the-world-are-you?!"* Her favorite thing in the world is her frisbee, and she has even managed to incorporate her frisbee fetish into her nursing home therapy as a way to give her nursing home friends valuable exercise and fun.

Miss June Bug showed signs as a precocious therapy dog early. Whereas some dogs shy away from wheel chairs, and from the persons in them, Buggie seemed drawn to them almost from the beginning. "My male Scottie doesn't like wheel chairs, and just isn't suited for therapy work," says Tunia Hyland, June Bug's owner. "But June Bug is one of those special dogs who seems to sense human need and suffering, and is drawn to those injured or handicapped. It's like she senses pain and wants to help."

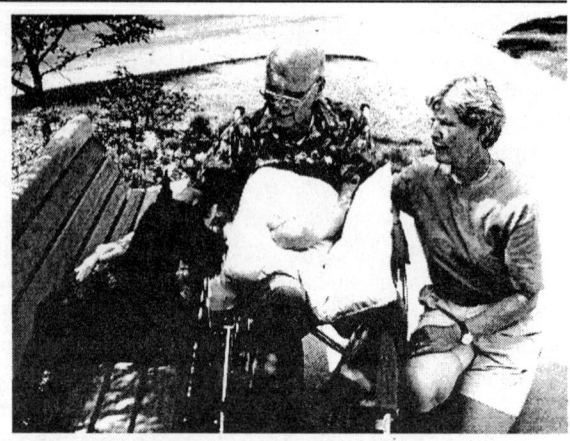

Miss June Bug, certified therapy dog, enjoys quiet-time with her special friend, Wesley. Owner Tunia Hyland, at right, says 'Buggy' is "a ministering angel to all who know her." Photo by Tunia Hyland.

And help she does in remarkable ways. In a Philadelphia psychiatric hospital she encountered a patient lying on the floor, withdrawn and non-communicative toward staff and visitors alike. June Bug proceeded to lick the patient's face thoroughly. The patient looked up and smiled— the first signs of interactivity some on the staff could remember. Tunia spoke to the patient saying, "Do you know why my dog loves you so much? Because you have a beard like hers!" The man laughed, and began to speak to June Bug and to Tunia.

June Bug has been in training of one kind or another since 4 months of age. She is a certified therapy dog, and recently has begun agility training. It is clear, however, that Buggie has a love of people that cannot be taught in obedience classes. At the nursing home where she now makes her weekly visits she brings a manifest magic to the wards and rooms where she is seen. "Passers-by stop in the halls to talk," says Tunia. "She's such a wonderful facilitator; she's like glue for bringing people together."

During her first year of therapy work with June Bug, Tunia worked under the auspices of an organization whose philosophy was minimal exposure to as many different patients as possible. June Bug saw each patient for about 5 minutes and then went on to the next room.

But this approach lacked opportunity for meaningful relationship, and Tunia and June Bug longed to give more. Tunia used her aging mother as a test case, asking her which she would prefer, a brief appearance or a 30 minute visit? Her mother was quick to say she would much rather look forward to a regular visit of significant duration from a dog she could get to know and enjoy. The outcome of Tunia's re-thinking of her therapy goals was the decision to do her therapy on her own in a form better suited to her's and June Bug's values. It would not be possible to visit everyone for 30 minutes each—neither Tunia nor June Bug were unrealistic about limitations. But it would be possible for June Bug and Tunia to focus their time and energy on someone with special needs, and cultivate a true relationship with that person. To the Hylands, at least, it made sense to bring real and substantial Scottie-therapy to one patient rather than superficial and marginal therapy to many who would remain largely strangers.

For the past year Miss June Bug has taken over the Scottie-care of a special new nursing home friend named Wesley. Wesley is a 75 year-old man who suffered a severe stroke two years ago that left him paralyzed on one side. June Bug and Tunia go for quality time with Wesley each week for half an hour or so, Buggie wearing her uniform consisting of a red backpack containing Scottie treats and her prized frisbee. Tunia wheels Wesley into the 'living room' where June Bug sits in a chair on Wesley's good side so he can pet Buggie for the first 15 minutes or so of the visit. And Miss June Bug knows

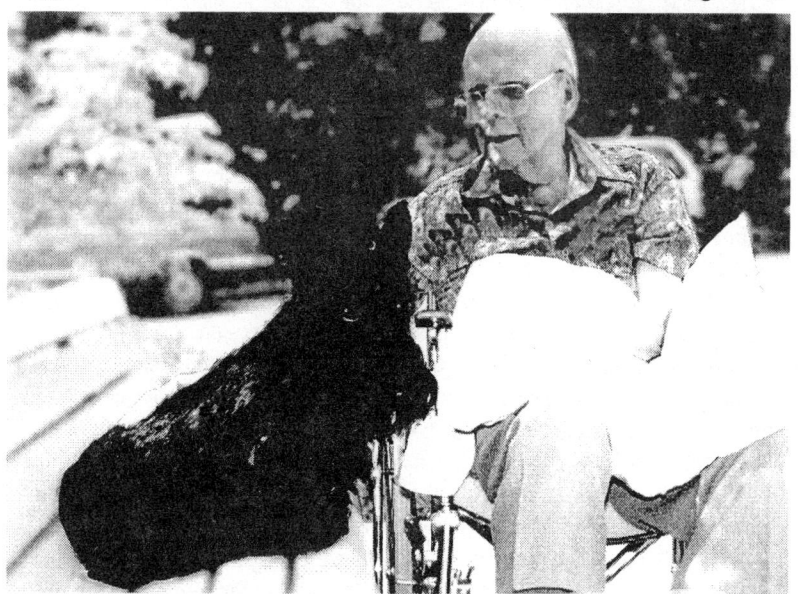

Tunia Hyland, June Bug's owner, believes nursing home residents prefer regular visits of significant duration from a dog so they get to know and truly enjoy the animal. 'Buggie' and her friend, Wesley, agree. Photo Tunia Hyland.

Miss June Bug, certified therapy dog, has learned to bring real and substantial Scottie-therapy to one patient rather than superficial and marginal therapy to many who remain largely strangers. Photo by Tunia Hyland.

how to enjoy strokes from her friends as well as how to give them! After their serious mutual 'strokes' given and received, Wesley throws June Bug's prized frisbee for 15 minutes of non-stop fun. It is not easy to estimate who gets the greater pleasure out of this exercise, since both therapist and patient appear to draw strength from the joy of their shared frisbee ritual.

These weekly visits have come to mean a lot to Wesley. Like many males of his generation, he is not an emotive man— he doesn't show his feelings easily to friends or family. And it took 3-4 months for Miss June Bug to work her magic on him. But today, as soon as Wesley sees his personal Scottie angel, he lights up. Despite his paralysis, which makes it difficult to hold up his head or do many of the other body movements we take for granted, when he sees June Bug his head raises up and he begins to smile and to talk and to express his affection for his special Scottie friend.

I asked Tunia what she gets out of these therapy sessions. She made it clear that to her mind she is the beneficiary, getting far more than she gives from both Wesley and June Bug. "When I go with her," Tunia says, "she gives me confidence. It's so heart-warming to see smiles on otherwise passive faces, and to know that I have a part in giving Wesley something really special to look forward to. Seeing June Bug work her magic with Wesley and others makes me appreciate my Scottie so much. She's taught me much more than I've ever taught her. She's so patient and gentle, so non-judgmental. She has no prejudices so she overlooks stains and spills and odors or other surface features which color how we humans see and treat each other. June Bug has taught me a great deal about what it means to love and be a friend."

Tunia has trained June Bug to give Wesley a "high five" when it is time to leave. Buggie assumes the classic Scottie begging pose and waves her paw for Wesley to "give her five!"

But in Bryn Mawr, Pennsylvania, this little Scottie angel is giving her friend Wesley, and all the rest of us, a lot more than a parlor trick. She is giving us a profound object lesson in how love sees beneath life's scars and heals the broken spirit.

---

*This chapter is a revision of an article originally published under the same title by Joseph Harvill, in *GSM*, Vol 2 No 4 (Jul/Aug) 1997.

CHAPTER TWENTY

Zoe:
God's Administrative Assistant

People go to church for many reasons. Some seek forgiveness, some search for answers, some go out of duty. In Sapulveda, California, the homeless go for a 'blessing' from Zoe.

Zoe is a nine year-old Scottie who is the secret weapon in the fight to 'rescue the perishing' at the local United Methodist Church. To young and old alike in Sapulveda, Zoe is heaven's "administrative assistant" who has a way with saints and sinners that opens heaven's gates.

Zoe, you see, knows something about 'rescuing the perishing,' since she herself is a rescue dog. "She was turned over to Carol Herd at the Southern California Scottie Rescue program when she was 13 months old," reports Pam Trickett, Zoe's owner and UMC church secretary. "When I got her she weighed just 10 pounds! Today, after eight years, she's still small at 17 lbs, but despite her rough beginnings, she loves everybody and has the biggest heart in the world!"

Zoe goes to 'her' church office every day, accompanied by her 'assistant,' Pam Trickett. "It's not me visitors ask about first when they come to the office," says Pam. "It's, 'Where's Zoe?' and 'How's Zoe, today?'" And Zoe has her own way of making every visitor feel special: she stretches up to them,

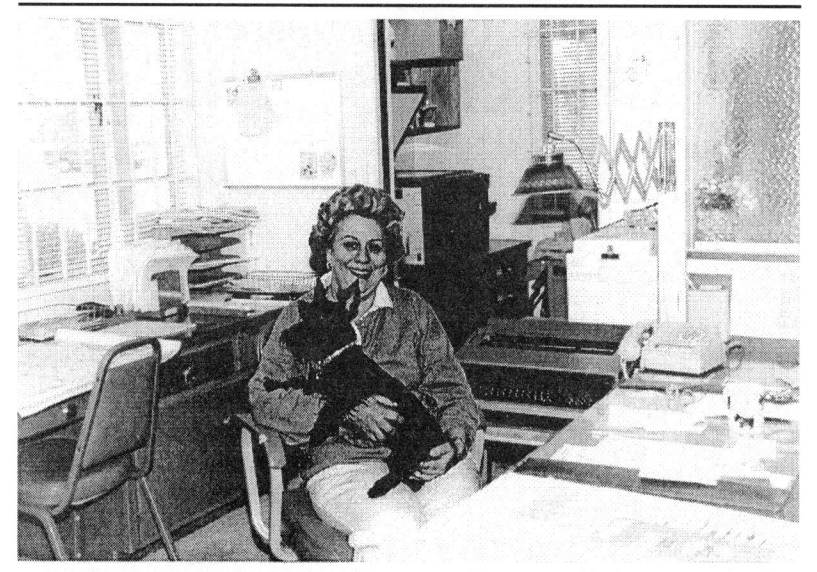

Pam Trickett, Administrative Assistant for the United Methodist Church, Sapulveda, CA., in the church office with 9 year-old Zoe, the congregation's much-loved canine ambassador. Photo: Pam Trickett.

forepaws reaching up for affection, which she gets and lavishly returns. Zoe transforms every stranger into an instant 'believer'— at least into a believer in her charms as church ambassador!

Pam says a typical day for Zoe at the church office begins in the early morning when she greets the Headstart children as they arrive for Day School. Then it is welcoming the homeless who come for the church's hot breakfast program. An almost daily ritual consists of homeless regulars entering the church office with the announcement, "I need to see my dog!" And Zoe makes each one feel ownership, too. "She is absolutely without prejudice," observes Pam. "She truly loves everybody, unconditionally, and they know it."

Zoe is a smiler whose favorite spot is atop Pam's desk in the center of the church office! "I have the ultimate Scottie paper weight," Pam insists. Recently a caller on the telephone asked Pam to consult her church calendar, and when the caller heard what sounded like inordinate paper shuffling on Pam's end of the line, she commented that Pam's desk sounded as cluttered as her's. "You don't understand," replied Pam. "I have a Scottish Terrier curled up on my desk!" Twenty minutes later there was a knock at Pam's church office door. It was the caller who said, "I just had to come right over to see if you were telling me the truth!"

Zoe accompanies Pam wherever she goes on her daily rounds as church secretary. And Zoe's right there for worship on Sunday morning, too. Right in the front pew. And no one in the congregation thinks anything about it. Zoe is an important part of their spiritual world.

Not every church, of course, is ready for Scotties on Sunday. But, then, the Sapulveda United Methodist Church is no ordinary church. Like Saint Francis, they have a long history of loving animals as well as humans. Seeing-eye dogs in training have been fostered by members, and creatures of all kinds over the years have been loved as mascots. So Zoe's presence at church functions is not only normal at this church, it is vital.

Only visitors seem to notice. Recently an out of town visitor came rushing up to Pam after the Sunday service to verify what his eyes could not believe: a Scottie dog front and center at worship! "This has to be the most amazing church I've ever seen!," he exclaimed as he shared warm greetings with Zoe. The Scottie, of course, spiritual maven that she is, could not understand what all the theological wonderment was about!

Because Zoe is a giver she fits right into the great-souled spirit of the Sapulveda congregation. One particular story says it all. That day things were busier than usual at the church because a funeral service was scheduled in the sanctuary. A much-loved grandmother in the congregation had died and her open-casket service was in progress. Pam became aware that Zoe was not in the office. Pam went looking for her Scottie but could not find her anywhere. Finally, she peeked into the sanctuary and there were Zoe's two pointy ears front and center above the pew in her place. Zoe had gone to pay her respects to her friend. The family later told Pam that during the service Zoe walked down the center aisle, went straight up to the casket, paused quietly, then turned and jumped into her pew. "Grandmother loved animals," the family said. "She would be so pleased that Zoe came to say good-bye!"

The old question, what is in a name?, seems to

Zoe, front and center, with Pam Trickett (left) and a young friend, at Sunday worship. Photo: Pam Trickett.

find clear answer in this little Scottie. You see 'zoe' in biblical Greek means "life" in the sense of the dynamics of the good life. It is the word St. John uses in the Fourth Gospel in the phrase "eternal life." In biblical terms, 'zoe' is not mere breath and existence, but life in the full sense of life-with-heavenly-meaning.

And *life-with-heavenly-meaning* is precisely what a little Scottie dog brings daily to the lives of young and old, to both haves and have-nots, in Sapulveda, California. With her irresistible Scottie charm Miss Zoe opens wide heaven's gates by her gifts of unconditional love.

Zoe, the church-dog, at 'her' congregation in Sapulveda, CA. Photo: Pam Trickett.

---

*This chapter is a revision of an article originally published under the same title by Joseph Harvill, in *GSM*, Vol 4 No 4 (Jul/Aug) 1999.

Pam Trickett is no longer employed at the Sepulveda, CA., United Methodist Church. She and Zoe, however, continue as 'ministering angels' to all who know them.

CHAPTER TWENTY-ONE

Shorty: The Infantry Mascot Who Fought in WWII

It is wicked to romanticize war. There is nothing romantic about the sight, sound, and smell of wounded men dying. To those who've been there it is not romantic; it is hell.

Yet from the battle fields of WWII comes a little-known story, redolent with affections of the heart, of a much-loved Scottie among the men of Company "G" 133rd Infantry Regiment, part of the "Red Bull" Division which had the most days in combat of any American division; the true story of a Scottie named "Shorty" whose presence was a welcome piece of home and affection in the killing fields of war.

Shorty's story comes from the source, his master Anver Habhab, a decorated soldier who in 1988 self-published a tribute to the little Scottie who went to war with him in 1940. The dog was smuggled on and off troopships in Habhab's duffle bag, became the darling of Company "G's" cook who always made sure Shorty ate well, and as adopted mascot of the infantry company recruited out of Fort Dodge, Iowa, became canine witness to some of the bloodiest fighting of the war.

Shorty's story begins in Detroit, Michigan, in 1938 in the home of Anver

Habhab's brother, Shafee. When Shafee brought the pup to Fort Dodge for a family visit, Shorty took up instantly with Shafee's kid brother, Anver, and when he returned to Detroit Shafee made his little brother a present of the dog. Even WWII could not keep Anver and Shorty apart after that!

Anver Habhab's shop-keeper parents immigrated from Syria before WWI, and by hard work became successful store owners in Iowa. His parents presented Anver with his own small grocery store as a graduation present when he finished high school. It was in that store that young Shorty began his 'training' in subterfuge which later served him well in the war. It seems the local health inspector at Fort Dodge took offense at a dog's daily presence in Anver's store, and told Habhab to lose the dog or lose his food license! After that encounter Anver trained Shorty to run and hide whenever the inspector approached, and it was not long until Shorty himself recognized the steps and sight of the inspector and would quickly hide himself! The precocious little Scottie was an adaptive genius.

When President Roosevelt pushed through the Selective Service Act in 1940 and Anver knew he would be called up, he decided to close his store and enlist along with three of his hometown buddies in Company "G" of the 34th Division National Guard Infantry Regiment being formed at Fort Dodge.

Anver's first training was at the local armory and Shorty went along to watch the marching drills. When he did not approve of something Shorty would bark from the sidelines, and someone in the company would say,

Shorty, the Iowa Scottie who witnessed some of the bloodiest fighting of WWII sits on his duffel bag in which owner, Anver Habhab, smuggled him on and off troopships. Photo by Anver Habhab.

Shorty and Anver home on leave in Fort Dodge, IA., c. 1942. Photo: A. Habhab.

"Now Sergeant Shorty's giving orders!" From the start Shorty was a hit with the new recruits, especially with Johnny, one of Anver's close friends, who became a cook in the company's kitchen and always looked out for Shorty throughout the war.

After Pearl Harbor Company G was mobilized in February 1942, and shipped out to Camp Claiborne, Louisiana. As a green private Anver was in awe of Army brass and was afraid to ask if Shorty could go along. Shorty stayed home.

But that soon changed. Anver's first furlough home convinced him he missed Shorty too much. The little dog followed him around the house and never let him out of his sight. Anver decided he would rather seek the army's forgiveness than its permission, so when he returned to Camp Claiborne, Shorty went with him.

Turns out Shorty took to Army life better than Anver. When he arrived at Camp Claiborne he sniffed the bunks inside Anver's barracks tent, found Anver's cot and planted himself under it. Shorty was in the Army now! The open air of field training suited Shorty just fine. On long hikes he would trot along beside Anver, and when he got tired he would display his Scottie 'majesty' by falling out and finding a shady bush or tree! At that point Anver or one of his buddies would fall out of ranks, pick Shorty up, and carry him atop his back pack. And, of course, Shorty's friend, Johnny, the company cook, always made sure the little Scottie from Fort Dodge had choice pieces of people food.

In early 1942 the 34th Division received overseas orders, first stop Fort

Shorty hitches a ride on Anver's pack

Private Anver Habhab and Shorty at Camp Claiborne, LA. Below Shorty sits at the barracks door behind Sergeant Coats.

*Photo credit: from Anver Habhab, **Shorty at War, 1941-1945**. Fort Dodge, IA, 1988.*

Dix, New Jersey. Shorty made the long train trip just fine, attending to nature's calls by being dropped from the coach window whenever the steam engine stopped to take on water, and then returning to the train steps when finished to be hoisted aboard by his soldier friends. It was winter in New Jersey and water froze inside canteens in the barracks tents. Shorty slept between the blankets on Anver's cot.

Knowing they were going overseas, Anver phoned his brother, Shafee, in Detroit to come get Shorty. He came for a few days' visit and as the time to leave drew closer Anver grieved at the thought of leaving his Scottie behind. They devised a plan to permit Shorty himself to settle the question, should Shorty go or stay? They each took ten steps away from the dog and on signal they both whistled for Shorty to come. Whoever Shorty went to was where he would go. Shorty went overseas.

Anver knew he would have to smuggle Shorty on board the troopship so he began training him to curl up and lie quietly inside his barracks bag. To make room for him in his kit bag Anver's buddies each took a few of his belongings. When finally Anver could jostle, roll and manhandle the barracks bag without a sound from the little dog inside, he knew he was ready. At the

New York Port of Embarkation, with his barracks bag over his shoulder and Shorty curled up quietly inside, Anver walked up the gangplank past the grim-faced MPs without a hitch.

After the ship cleared the harbor Anver let Shorty out of the bag. A ship's officer soon spotted him and demanded explanation from Anver. Scooping up Shorty into his arms, Anver answered, "What do you want me to do, throw him overboard?" The solemn-faced officer's eyes met Shorty's. There was a breathless moment. Then the officer turned and walked away. Shorty had the run of the ship.

Shorty entered North Ireland as he left New York: smuggled inside Anver's barracks bag. Shorty and the men of Company "G" went to Limavady, and then to Walworth, and then to Caledon in North Ireland. At Caledon Shorty and Anver became close friends with Mary McGinnis whose local pub had been in the family since the 17th century. Like the old days at Anver's grocery, Shorty and Anver once hid under the staircase to escape roving MP's checking curfew.

Anver was assigned company jeep driver during rigorous training in Ireland, England, and Scotland. Shorty rode regally in the back seat while passengers rode in the front.

In 1943 Company "G" was chosen as part of the 133rd Infantry to guard General Eisenhower's Allied Headquarters in North Africa. So Anver and Shorty became part of the "Palace Guards" in Algiers. Shorty met General Eisenhower and received a commending pat from the Scottie-lover General for being a

Shorty goes "pub crawling" with Anver and Company "G" buddies in Caledon, North Ireland. Proprietor, Mary McGuinnis, third from left.

Clifford Sabine, a Company "G" buddy, with Shorty in Algiers, North Africa.

good soldier. Shorty met Ike's Scottie, too, and played for half an hour with Telek, any question of rank being quite moot!

When Eisenhower returned to England in 1944 to direct the invasion of Europe Shorty and Company "G" sailed to Italy for strenuous combat training. On March 25, 1944, they headed for the Anzio beachhead, the bloody scene where in January American and British infantry had fought a terrible invasion battle. Although the main invasion fighting was over, the Germans were dug in so that holding the narrow strip of Allied beachhead was done under artillery fire and air raids.

Anver's company went straight to the front. Johnny in the kitchen agreed to take care of Shorty. The kitchen area was located about two miles behind the front, but it, too, was exposed to artillery fire. Shorty coped with the shellfire but air raids frightened him. The scream of fighter engines told him what was coming. He would stand still and shiver with his little ears back until a kind GI would pick him up and comfort him.

At night the kitchen crew brought food and ammunition to the front line (and took back the dead). Shorty would come with Johnny, and Anver and Shorty would eat together at the kitchen truck. Shelling, bombing, skirmishes and patrols continued around the clock at Anzio. Combined American losses before the breakout were 2,800 killed and 11,000 wounded.

The breakout came in May, 1944, after Shorty had been on the line 69 days. As part of the 34th "Red Bull" Division, Company "G" began its drive to Rome, part of the agonizing, Allied blood-letting that was the Italian campaign. At times the kitchen crew was so far in the rear Anver and his buddies were forced to eat K-rations and forage the countryside. But worse than being without hot food, separation from the kitchen unit meant Anver could not see Shorty.

Company "G" and the "Red Bull" Division reached Rome in June, 1944, and were cheered by exuberant Italians throwing flowers and kisses. Anver and Shorty got to stay just long enough to march through it. On June 6th they were pursuing retreating Germans northwest of the city.

The Italian campaign has been described by General Bolte, who became

Commander of the 34th Division in July, as "the caldron of Italy." Allied casualties were terribly high. There were consecutive days when Company "G" averaged 10 killed and 40 wounded. Replacements often were killed their first day in the line. Platoon leaders and squad sergeants were especially vulnerable. In Company "G" fellow private Lyman Woodard and Anver were two of those who had leadership thrust upon them. Casualties quickly made them acting squad sergeants and then platoon sergeants. Anver, showing the diehard spirit of his beloved Scottie, rose to the challenge again and again, with initiative and courage in battles for which the Army awarded him the Silver Star.

On July 17th in the vicinity of San Carlos, Italy, Anver was hit by machine gun fire. Two bullets shattered his right arm and three more shattered his left. Miraculously, none hit the rest of him! Pinned down by ferocious German fire in front, and by Allied artillery and mortar fire from the slope behind, Anver and the other wounded were in grave need of medical attention. A ceasefire was called to the regimental command post; the Germans reciprocated; medics and stretcher-bearers on both sides collected the dead and dying off the bloody battlefield.

Anver was evacuated to a hospital in Rome and then transferred to Naples to await a hospital ship home. Wounded and in great pain in a body cast, let down after the adrenalin rush of battle and far from the comaraderie of war buddies, he was half conscious in his hospital bed and kept asking for Shorty.

Meanwhile, Shorty nervously greeted all who came out of the line from Company "G" desperately looking for Anver to return. One by one he went to Anver's buddies searching in vain for the man he loved. He was talked to and comforted, and told Anver would be okay, but he only whimpered and became disconsolate. Always before when Anver was away Shorty adjusted. This time he sensed something more.

When the battalion commander, Lt. Col. B.G. Marchi, heard how Shorty grieved for his master he detailed a driver to take Shorty 200 miles to the Naples hospital, and in so doing, sent better 'medicine' to Anver Habhab than was available to medical science. At the hospital at last, Shorty paused to look down the long ward of wounded men on cots, saw Anver's smiling face at the far end, and trotted to his cot wagging his tail. After subdued 'hellos' which only a Scottie lover comprehends as the way of this deeply sensitive but reserved breed, Shorty studied Anver's face, then, satisfied, stretched out on the floor alongside him. Shorty's world was right once again.

It was the hospital orderlies who came up with the solution to the dilemma how to smuggle Shorty aboard the hospital ship home. With both arms in casts the barracks bag over the shoulder ruse was out. Anver was converted to a litter patient and they hid Shorty under the blankets. MP's routinely searched GIs on the lookout for guns being smuggled home, so Anver worried how he

Anver Habhab and Shorty during convelescence at Percy Jones Hospital, Battle Creek, MI. Below: Shorty's brass membership tag to the 34th Division Association.

would keep Shorty from being discovered.

For three long hours Anver and Shorty lay on the dock waiting to board. The Scottie angels smiled on the pair once again, when the officious MPs missed—or overlooked—Shorty.

In the States, wounded soldiers were privileged citizens, and Anver was permitted to keep Shorty with him for his long convelescence at Percy Jones Hospital in Battle Creek, Michigan. As it happened, Anver and Shorty were home on furlough to Fort Dodge, Iowa, on VJ Day and Shorty was the war hero and honored occupant of a parade convertible through town.

Anver was released from hospital and went home for good on Christmas Eve 1946. He opened the 34th Division Key Club Bar in Fort Dodge. Shorty was awarded a brass card of membership in the 34th Division Association as a "Life Member" and Number 1 Canine, and honored in newspaper tributes.

Having gone through six years in the military, a silent witness to some of WWII's bloodiest European fighting, Shorty died in 1950 in Anver's arms at age 12. Anver's brother, Shafee, was there to cry with his brother as he said goodbye to the little Iowa Scottie who brought a bit of home and humanity to the dogfaces of Company "G" through all the madness of war.

> *"Well, old vets never die — they just fade from our view, and I've got to believe it's the same for dogs, too. When that Great General musters his brave 'Red Bull' men they'll see Anver and Shorty — together again!"*

Anonymous Tribute to Shorty

This *GSM* version of the Shorty story is based on Anver Habhab's book, ***Shorty at War, 1941-1945***, which was self-published at Fort Dodge, IA., 1988. This chapter first appeared under this title in *GSM*, Vol 5 No 3 (May/Jun) 2000. While there are better known Scotties of WWII none exceeded the danger or the devotion of Shorty. His story is one of the great companionship stories of all time.

Part Three:
Celebrating the Scottie Good Life

Redeeming the Shadows

> *"The misery of keeping a dog is his dying so soon. But to be sure, if he lived for fifty years and then died, what becomes of me?"*
>
> Sir Walter Scott

CHAPTER TWENTY-TWO

Why Do I Hurt So Much?— A Look Inside the Pain of Scottie Loss

The pain of 'good-byes' is nothing new. Homer knew something of this pain and had the Greek hero, Odysseus, and his dog, Argos, model for all time in *The Odyssey* the pathos of the ancient Graecian experience. Odysseus had been away for 20 years, long given-up for dead by his family and friends. Disguised, he returned to his homeland to find interlopers conspiring for his lands and his wife. His appearance had changed after so many perils, so many years, and no one recognized him—except his dog, Argos. He knew his master's voice, the sound of which, after so long a wait, validated the dog's loyalty, and seemed to grant old Argos release from his faithful vigil. Odysseus knew the grief. So did Homer.

In ancient Egypt when one's cat died the owner shaved off their eye brows in a ritual of mourning. When their dog died, they shaved their entire body.

What is new today at the start of the 21st century is not grief over the loss of pets. In every age those who truly bonded have known the pain of grieving over their dog's death. However, because of psycho-social factors in our era, I believe our sense of loss is significantly compounded. These cultural changes hold important clues why saying goodbye to Scottie companions is such a crisis for contemporary Scottie lovers, and point us toward understanding which can aid healing.

Today's Pain

It is my belief that today's grief over lost pets is both more widespread and more acute than ever before in canine-human history. Odysseus' "salt tear" over Argos, carefully concealed from his peers, is replaced in our culture by an avalanche of public mourning. There is today an International Association of Pet Cemeteries that lists 100 member locations across the country, who pledge "to help other people and their family pet members, by providing sincere, realistic pet 'after care'." Says Joe Haswell, past director of Hillside Acres Cemetery near Boston, "You ought to see this place on Memorial Day. There are more people over here than over at the human cemetery." There is even a pet cemetery in Baltimore, Maryland, that permits pets and their owners to be buried in adjacent plots. Even cyberspace has become an arena for pet mourning and grief. Sites have proliferated in recent years such as **The Virtual Pet Cemetery** @ *http://www.lavamind.com/pet.html*, where grieving pet owners post online pet memorials for all the world to see.

So radically changed is the family status accorded today's household pet that it is not uncommon for persons to grieve more intensely over the death of a pet than over the loss of a relative. The reason, affirms a Massachusetts social worker, is "... our (pet) love and then our grief are pure." Bob Barton,

---

> "While he spoke an old hound, lying near, pricked up his ears and lifted up his muzzle. This was Argos, trained as a puppy by Odysseus, but never taken on a hunt before his master sailed for Troy ... Treated as rubbish now, he lay at last upon a mass of dung before the gates ... Abandoned there, and half destroyed with flies, old Argos lay.
>
> But when he knew he heard Odysseus' voice nearby, he did his best to wag his tail, nose down, with flattened ears, having no strength to move nearer his master. And the man looked away, wiping a salt tear from his cheek; but he hid this from Eumaios ... but death and darkness in that instant closed the eyes of Argos, who had seen his master, Odysseus, after twenty years."
>
> *The Odyssey*, Book XVII (trans. Robt. Fitzgerald)

The largest pet cemetery in the U.S.A., the Hartsdale Canine Pet Cemetery, Hartsdale, NY. Source: Hartsdale Canine Pet Cemetery, Hartsdale, NY.

proprietor of W.N.C. Marble and Granite Company, of Marble, NC., agrees:

"I've watched big, strong men, who didn't shed a tear at the funeral of a relative, break down and cry their eyes out when ordering one of our gravestones for their deceased dog. It's different with pets. Our dogs love us unconditionally; humans don't."

Dog Power

Recent historical research analyzing what Mary Thurston calls "our 15,000-year love affair with dogs," has documented the dramatic rise in the social status of the dog in modern times. The ubiquitous family dog is major business in our culture, and the household Scottie is royalty.

What this new family status means is that the bonding between dogs and humans which in earlier times was the privilege of the few, has now become the experience of the masses. And this means the grieving over lost bonds of companionship once confined to royalty and the rich is now experienced in the population at large. Our grief may not be new, but it is more widespread than ever before in history.

Hyper Pain

But there is more to our grief crisis than rising numbers of those experiencing it. Today's sense of loss is more acute and traumatic.

Researchers have found that grief levels are directly affected by the level of attachment of the caretaker with the animal, the suddenness of the animal's death, and whether or not the person lives alone.

The dramatic rise in the attachment status of contemporary family pets since WWII, together with the aging of our population and rising numbers of those living alone, indicate why our culture is singularly situated for extraordinary grief levels.

The relevance of this for Scottie lovers is that everything that can be posited of the general population's new attachment to dogs and the attendant social consequences, must be compounded by a factor of 10 when assessing what Scottie people know as "the Scottie Crazies." In Scottie circles attachments that elsewhere would be extraordinary are not remarkable at all; they are the norm. This suggests that because our attachments are extraordinary, our grieving will be extraordinary as well.

Going Deeper

But modern attachment levels to our dogs are themselves effects produced by deeper cultural changes. Why, after all, are we so attached to our Scotties? There are three larger societal changes which drive our attachments and which profoundly deepen our sense of loss when our Scotties die.

The first of these deeper cultural changes is the shrinking of the family. Quite literally the size of the average American household today is half the size it was 50 years ago. And counting the number of heads present doesn't begin to assess the profounder psychological shrinking of the extended family and its attendant loss of network and sense of belonging.

Upward mobility and career migrations over the past two generations carried the hidden costs of broken ties to place and heritage and loss of the rootedness and attachments which shaped and sustained earlier generations. Today we compensate for our rootlessness by elevating the mini-world of our immediate family— including especially our Scotties— to new levels of pride and importance. The selfhood that in the past was vouchsafed by continuity of time and place, today is dependent upon the fragile threads of jobs and immediate relationships.

Experts say there is an inverse correlation between the size of the tribe and the crisis surrounding death— the smaller the group the more threatening it is to lose a group member.

Because we have traded the mobile nuclear family for the rooted extended family of agrarian times we set ourselves up for great difficulty dealing with death within our shrunken family unit. And when one of our members dies, the loss is disproportionately

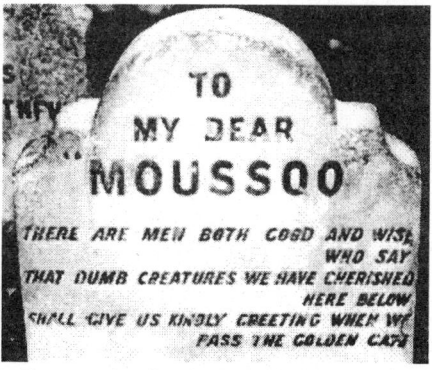

Victorian-era headstone in Hyde Park Dog Cemetery, London, England.

Hyde Park Dog Cemetery headstone.

devastating and we hurt a lot.

Shattered Myths

The second of the deeper cultural factors which ratchets up our grief over the death of our Scotties is modern myths about science and technology. Myth, in the technical sense, refers to the collective consciousness of a people, to the communal sense of what-it-means-to-be-us, often embodied in the stories and icons of a culture.

American myth revolves around technology and competency. The whole globe envies the virtuosity of our science. We are believers in this myth of technology, too, and that is as true of the fundamentalist preacher whose ministry is dependent on high-tech telecommunications, as of the child learning to surf the internet. We make technology, then technology shapes our lives.

The trouble is today's glitzy special effects are so realistic and advances in science so amazing we foster the delusion that our technology is omnipotent and our scientific virtuosity unlimited. We are in control.

But the death of a beloved Scottie companion shatters the myth and our confidence, and awkwardly confronts us at painful existential levels with the truth of our personal powerlessness and mortality. Science is weak and clumsy in the face of death, and when it is defective or bungled science, it is death's terrifying accomplice.

To experience this helplessness in your bones as you watch your companion Scottie die is, in our culture, to lose more than companionship; it is to lose faith in our culture's gods.

Security Blanket

The third of the deeper cultural changes which exacerbates our grieving over the death of our Scotties is the unrecognized 'security blanket' syndrome in which we wrap our dogs today.

Psychologists have long recognized that pets hold significant roles in many children's lives as transitional objects to adulthood. Similar to the blanket that the toddler must have when it goes to sleep, the family dog, as loyal companion, helps youngsters find psychological anchor in the midst of change. This is why adolescents have a more difficult time than younger children in resolving grief over a pet's death— they have a shared history which is singularly tied up with their sense of who they are and what it means to be them.

What is not adequately recognized is the contemporary role of dogs as transitional objects for adults in our culture. Alvin Toffler, in his many books, has taught us what is overwhelming today is not merely the quantity of change all around us, but the unprecedented rapidity of change. He called it "future shock," and the notion of stunned disorientation is an apposite picture of the way many feel in today's world of prized gadgetry and throw-away relationships. A recent *New Yorker* cartoon pictured a professional in a job interview where the boss says, *"We expect little loyalty, and in return we offer little job security."* The brutal frankness here is both humorous and alarming.

Wrenching life-change, or the threat of it, is pervasive: in the job market, in our marriages and relationships, in our health, in our neighborhoods. And in the midst of all this future shock it is not just children who grope for some kind of security blanket.

In a profound sense today's unprecedented attachments to canines in general, and to Scotties in particular, reflect our adult gropings after security blankets to relieve the relentless shock of overwhelming change. Our Scotties' loyalty and devotion are oases of security in a world at risk. Today's pandemic loss of security, loss of relational glue, loss of innocency, and loss of connection to Nature leave us painfully in need of transitional objects to cushion the shock in our lives. Many find that object in their Scotties.

That is asking a great deal of our Scottie relationships— to virtually serve as surrogate nurturers in place of community and social structures which filled those roles in earlier times. It is a credit to our dogs' great-souled spirits that they so effectively rise to the demands of today's higher-order companionship.

Modern pet mummification, 'Egyptian Style,' of a dog named Butch, encased in a polished bronze sarcophagus. Source: Summum Mummification, Salt Lake City, UT.

But to see this new role for our Scottie relationships is to see clearly why losing them is such a blow. It's not just difficult; it means facing life without the one thing amidst all the craziness which made sense.

Conclusion

Saying good-bye has never been easy. And there are compelling reasons why it is harder today than ever. Our world of lost security, troubled relationships, lost innocency, and isolation from Nature, drives us to exceptional attachments, and to profound crisis surrounding death.

The elevation of Scotties to family status has brought rewards of profound companionship, but it also brings unprecedented grief. Because we think the world of our Scotties, it is our world which crashes when they are gone.

But that is love's price. Real love is not about risk management; not about rations and limits and holding back out of fear of pain. Love is about pouring it all out, and then wishing there were more to give.

Argos knew such devotion on the dung heap of ancient Ithaca. He loved even in disgrace to the very end.

And in the same way that Argos' sad plight in Homer's story mirrored Odysseus' tragedies, so today our Scotties and the way we bond with them tell much about our own spiritual and emotional evolution.

To love without reservation while knowing the end that awaits is the human predicament. It is also our noblest calling.

To the wise, the Scotties in our lives offer more than fidelity, consolation, and companionship. They offer a profound and challenging model of what it means to give your heart with little thought of return. Perhaps it is not too late for them to teach us in death some important truths about love and life.

Further Reading

Christine Adamec, *When Your Pet Dies: Dealing with Your Grief and Helping Your Children Cope*. NY: Berkley Books, 1996. 180 pp, pb. The best inexpensive resource on this topic. Marjorie Garber, *Dog Love*. NY: Simon & Schuster, 1996. 346 pp. Chapter 7 on 'Dog Loss' is excellent. This is a major work well worth reading and pondering. Elisabeth Kubler-Ross, *On Death and Dying*. NY: Macmillan, 1977 (many editions). 289 pp, pb. This is the seminal 'text' on death and dying (human) which launched the modern field of research and writing. Herbert A. Nieburg, Ph.D., & Arlene Fischer, *Pet Loss: A Thoughtful Guide for Adults and Children*. NY: HarperCollins, 1996 ed. 151 pp, pb. Useful section on 'frequently asked questions.' Mary Elizabeth Thurston, *The Lost History of the Canine Race: Our 15,000-Year Love Affair with Dogs*. Kansas City: Andrews & McMeel, 1996. 301 pp. Excellent chapter on pet death, and the best overall treatment of human-canine evolution I have read. Thurston loves dogs, writes eloquently, and has made a serious contribution in this book to all dog lovers. If you can afford only one book on canine history get this one. Alvin Toffler, *The Third Wave*. NY: Bantam, 1981. 537 pp, pb. This is Toffler's second book, and I believe, his best. Returning to it now almost 20 yrs after first reading it, I am amazed at his prescience. Toffler is the best 'map' I know to help you make sense of our modern maelstrom we call life. Lloyd M. Wendt, *Dogs, A Historical Journey: The Human/Dog Connection through the Centuries*. NY: Howell Books, 1996. 258 pp. Not as useful as Thurston, but sprinkled with fascinating historical detail.

CHAPTER TWENTY-THREE

A Love Letter
Lee Netzler

Thursday, August 25, 1994

Dear Mom,
Hope that you are well.
Yesterday I hiked Mount Audubon. I went up with Piper and came home alone.

The alarm went off at 5 am. I got up and shaved and showered and dressed. Then I loaded a small cooler and my backpack, which I had readied the previous evening, into the Jeep. Filled up the gas tank on the way to aunt Alice's restaurant.

After breakfast it took an hour to drive up to the Indian Peaks Wilderness Area. As the road began to climb into the foothills, a big orange-red sun was rising on the horizon behind me, a spectacular sight even in the rear view mirror. Passing Brainard Lake, we saw one lone fisherman casting flies. I drove a mile further to the trailhead and parked. Got the canteen from the cooler, hoisted my pack onto my back, and we started out on the trail to Mount Audubon at 7:15 am.

It is about a 3 3/4 mile hike to the top of Mount Audubon. The trail begins at 10,480 feet above sea level and the summit is at 13,223 feet, so the elevation gain is something over 2,700 feet.

The weather was absolutely perfect. The temperature was in the low 50's, and there was no breeze whatsoever. The sky was mostly covered with a transparent overcast, and the sun was already half shielded. I considered wearing my jacket, but didn't, because I knew that soon my efforts against the continual incline of the trail would keep me warm....

About 3 hours later we reached a small level area which is about a 10 minute hike from the summit. I stopped there, as I had been planning to do. While we paused, I thought about the many, many previous hikes that Piper and I had done together. I talked to him about them, just as I had talked to him throughout the morning as we worked our way up the trail to this small resting place. I let him know how I felt and that there wasn't anything much better that could happen to a person in life than sharing company with a good dog. I drank a can of pop from my pack and put my gear in order. After about 10 minutes I got myself together and we set out to complete the short distance to the summit.

We arrived at the top of Mount Audubon at 10:20. A brisk breeze was blowing. It was cool, but pleasant. I dropped my pack and took out the pictures of our first hike together to this summit 9 years ago. I cried a lot. I was glad we were alone, because for a time I wailed at the top of my lungs and just couldn't stop.

I hugged him and said everything I could think of to say to him, and then I sent his ashes flying free with many sweeps of my hands. I sat there by myself for awhile, and then gathered up my things and started down. It was 10:40.

The trip down was more numb stumbling along than it was a hike. As I reached the base of the dome area I met two ladies, both in their mid-20s, hiking up with a beautiful Irish Setter. I stopped them and asked a favor-- *"Could I please pet your dog?"* They saw my tears and distress and although surprised by that, they tried to console me.

The dog's name was Ruby. She was perhaps 3 or 4 years old, very well behaved, and friendly. I petted her for several minutes, all the while explaining to them why I was so upset. I showed them Piper's pictures. When I left them, they were crying nearly as much as I, but I know they felt a whole lot better about having Ruby than they did a few minutes earlier.

I passed some other uphill hikers in the next mile or so. I exchanged polite greetings without slowing down.

Further ahead, I noticed a man and a woman stopped on the trail. They had two chocolate-colored Labradors with them, which were prancing around and playing. As I approached, I could see that the couple would alternately drink from their canteens and then tip them so that the dogs could drink from them as well.

Their fussing and concern over their dogs really struck me and I was crying pretty hard by the time I reached them. It took a few minutes before I could talk, but when I was finally able to explain myself, they were both very comforting.

"Montana" was the oldest Lab, probably 7 or 8, and the other was their 'new' dog-- maybe a year old. The couple appeared to be in their early 30s, and although they told me all of their names, I just wasn't listening and only remember "Montana." While trying to console me, the lady told me that neither of them was interested in having children and that their dogs were their "kids." They seemed to understand me and were not bothered by my tears.

When I was a little more composed, they asked me about my dog and I showed them Piper's pictures and told them about him. They had hiked Mount Audubon previously and were familiar with it. The lady was enthusiastic about what I had done. She said it was well thought out and appropriate-- *"What a great idea"*-- was the way she put it. We talked a little longer and when I got myself somewhat collected I hugged the labs, thanked the couple for their understanding, and continued down the trail.

About 300 yards further along I heard a short "chirp-cooing" sound. I stopped and listened, already knowing what it was . . . I kept looking, seeing nothing, until finally one of the creatures moved. They were White-tailed Ptarmigans, year-round residents of the tundra and rarely-seen members of the grouse family, camoflaged to near invisibility by their brown-speckled coats. There were 4 of them-- one slightly larger than the others, so I guessed it was a hen with 3 chicks. Two were beside me, about 30 and 40 feet from the trail. The other two were below me on the trail, perhaps 50 feet ahead. . . . I stood motionless. Clearly it knew I was there, but was curious. It approached very slowly and very deliberately, taking each step with great care, as it came to investigate me. It kept looking me over, thoroughly examining me all the while it advanced. I stood perfectly still, moving nothing except my eyes to study the bird . . . [It] passed two feet from me, close enough so that I could easily have bent over and stroked it without moving a foot. I waited until the birds moved away, then continued downhill.

I passed the Buchanan trail junction and re-entered the forest. The trees thickened again as I reached the flatter ground.

The last mile seemed very long and I realized that I was extremely tired. I tripped and fell once, just as I had on the way up, but without damage.

At 12:55 pm I reached the parking area. I lifted off my pack and canteen, and after a long drink, stowed them in the Jeep.

The hike was finished.

It was the hardest hike I've ever done.

Please take care, Mom. I will try to write again soon.

Love,
Lee

---

*This chapter appeared in GSM, Vol 2 No 3, (May/Jun) 1997, and is a reprint, with permission, of an essay out of Lee Netzler, **Oh How My Piper Played**, Longmont, CO: Netzler Publishing, 1995. Copies of Netzler's book available from the author at 7 Dartmouth Circle, Longmont, CO 80503. (303) 772-1764.

CHAPTER TWENTY-FOUR

On Loving Angus:
A Journey of the Heart

Linda Hill

Angus MacTavish came into our lives in April 1990. He was a planned addition to our family, but I truly believe he was meant especially for us. He was not a 'rescue' dog in the official sense of a Scottie coming from an organized rescue group or shelter. His coming to live with us was the result of a chance reading of an ad in the newspaper. He had been picked up running loose in the streets by a compassionate young couple, and no one ever claimed him.

He was pitifully thin. His coat was so matted and full of burrs he had to be completely shaved except for his beautiful grey beard. Never for one moment did we imagine that that pitiful, dejected looking Scottie would turn into such a loving, devoted and charming companion.

He joined my husband Bill and me and our then one year old female Scottie, Sheena, and became an integral part of our family. He lived with us for seven years and one day, and added immeasurable happiness to our lives.

On April 27, 1997, he finally lost his battle with three major diseases and we had to make the heartbreaking decision to have him put to sleep. We loved him deeply, and greatly mourn his passing.

I was working on an article for ***Great Scots Magazine*** on the topic of living with a terminally ill Scottie when Angus died. In order to do justice to this magnificent little Scottie I have abandoned the format of a formal article which I had begun and, instead, I have written a letter to Angus so that I can best communicate some of my many wonderful memories of and feelings for him.

TO OUR BELOVED ANGUS -- I will never forget:

♦ The look of fear and confusion in your eyes when I first saw you.

♦ The gentle kiss on the nose you gave me when I picked you up to take you home that day.

♦ The indignities you suffered at the hand of Sheena. We mistakenly assumed she would be delighted by your arrival, but at first she resented you terribly.

♦ The time before she finally accepted you that Sheena bit you, and I used peroxide to clean your wound, accidentally dying a red circle on your side!

♦ How frightened you were of men when you came to live with us. You would become so panicked if Bill walked toward you that you would fall down in your effort to get out of his way. Looking back it is hard to believe that he would become the person you would love and trust the most. The two

Angus MacTavish Hill. Photo: Linda Hill.

of you became almost inseparable. In my mind I can still picture you sitting on the den floor facing Bill cocking your head from side to side as he talked to you. Your serious and intent expression seemed to say, "I understand exactly what you mean!"

♦ You didn't know how to play until we taught you. How many times we wished you could tell us about your past. Perhaps it is best that you couldn't. Some of what you apparently suffered would have broken our hearts.

♦ The horrible nightmares that plagued you in your early years with us.

♦ Your terrible fear of abandonment. Something in your past left such deep scars that any activity resembling moving would send you into panic. My deepest sadness is losing you before we could erase all the fears of your past. Perhaps they never could have been.

♦ My anger and disbelief that any human could have mistreated you in any way.

♦ How you loved to ride in the car. Every Saturday when you heard the sound of Bill's electric razor, you would station yourself either at the bathroom or garage doors. You wanted to make sure you were positioned so that he couldn't possibly forget to invite you to run errands with him!

♦ Your passion for walking. You would sit in front of me when I came home from work, and stare me down until I relented and spoke those magic words, "Do you want to go walk?" When we walked, only people with the hardest of hearts would fail to eventually smile at the sight of the two of you sweeping down the sidewalk in tandem like twin dustmops.

- You and Sheena sitting side by side in the backyard on warm summer days looking like a pair of bookends while on lizard patrol.
- The way you loved to harrass the turtles in the yard. You would wait for one to crawl onto the concrete, and then would charge across the yard growling fiercely and hit your victim with your nose, spinning him in circles. Somehow I suspect the turtles do not miss you!
- The way you would tease Sheena in the morning when she was groggy. You figured out that she wouldn't retaliate at that hour, and you would charge at her repeatedly barking and playfully nipping at her nose. It irritated her no end, but she never would stand up to you in her sleepy state.
- The frenzy of excitement you would go into when we came home from work. No matter how hard our day may have been at the office, your warm and enthusiastic greeting made the problems of the day seem far distant.
- The many trips we took as a family, both for fun, and later for your medical problems.
- Your deep love of your home and family.
- Your sweet and affectionate nature. You never left any doubts in our minds that you loved us. You were a real snuggler, and always wanted to be touching one of us. If we became busy with some chore and ignored you for any period of time, you would quietly remind us of your presence by one gentle touch on the leg with your cold nose.
- The warmth of you leaned up against my legs at night, and the way you would growl if one of us happened to turn over in bed without giving you warning.
- The way you would occasionally throw your head back and give a mournful howl that would rival any Bloodhound when a siren would sound. I will never forget the first time you did it. We could not believe a Scottie could make such a sound!
- Your dignified bearing and your beautiful long grey beard. Combined, they earned you the nickname of "The Judge" among our friends.
- Your unfailing loyalty and forgiving spirit.
- The only time that you publicly embarrassed us. We took you and Sheena to PetsMart to have your picture taken with Santa Claus. You were both very good while waiting in line, but when our turn came we were horrified when you calmly walked over and lifted your leg on Santa's boot! Fortunately, Santa had the Christmas spirit and didn't get upset.
- The happy and handsome dog that you gradually turned into. You always threw yourself wholeheartedly into whatever you were doing, and enjoyed life to the fullest. How satisfying it was to see that early look of fear in your eyes turn into a look of contentment, devotion, and trust.
- The way you served as a goodwill ambassador for the Scottish Terrier breed throughout your life with us. Your gentleness, good behavior, and sweet and happy character impressed all who met you. Over and over both friends and strangers referred to you as a fine little gentleman.
- The times you and Sheena were invited to St. John's Episcopal School in Odessa to kick-off the reading of the "Angus" books by Marjorie Flack. How proud we were of the way you both behaved in the classroom. You were a big hit each visit. While there, Sheena would always end up romping in the middle of a group of loud excited children. You could usually be found sitting quietly wrapped in the arms of one of the most bashful children in the class. Your keen instincts seemed to tell you who could use a little extra attention.
- The serious devotion you gave to the role you assumed as supervisor of

the barbecue pit and kitchen.

♦ Your intense love of your things. Your soft white afghan traveled thousands of miles with us. In your early days, you had a ridiculous looking soft rubber green frog with a top-hat and cigar. You carried him everywhere with you until he eventually disintegrated from wear.

♦ Your valiant and courageous battle over a four year period, first against heart problems, then Cushing's disease, and finally the cancer that eventually claimed your life.

♦ The wonderful care you received at the Texas A&M University Veterinary School and the many times we made the long trip there.

The author's other Scottie, Sheena (left) and Angus. Since writing the original tribute to Angus in 1997, Sheena, too, has gone to the Rainbow Bridge. Photo: Linda Hill.

♦ Your patience and good nature in enduring a multitude of tests and procedures, especially the last two years of your life.

♦ The agony of giving permission for a portion of your jawbone to be removed in hopes of arresting your cancer.

♦ The change in Sheena as she became your protector and guardian when you were ill. She couldn't possibly have understood your jaw surgery, but she never tried to play tug of war with you again after it. She would immediately surrender any toy she was holding if you wanted to play with it. She is quite lost now without you.

♦ The deep and special bond that developed between us the last months of your life. We nearly lost you on Christmas Day, but were given a miraculous gift of four more months. As you became weaker and required more help, you accepted our assistance with grace, dignity, and gratitude.

Angus, my sweet little fellow, you were greatly loved by us, and it was our honor and privilege to be your people. Throughout your life you admirably lived up to the meaning of your Scottish name-- 'noble valor.' We were frequently asked if we would take you in again if we had known in advance the amount of time and heavy expense that your health problems would require, and the answer was always a resounding, "Absolutely!" No price tag could possibly be put on the love and happiness you gave to us. Your passing has left a void in our hearts, our home, and our lives. You will never be forgotten.

In the end, Angus became a rescue dog in the 'official' sense in that our love of him has gotten us involved in the wonderful work of Scottie rescue. It is a cause that I urge each of you to give to, in whatever way you can-- either time, monetary assistance, volunteer grooming, assistance transporting a dog, temporarily foster-homing a dog, or most importantly by giving a place in your home and heart to one of these needy and deserving animals.

It is our sincere wish that all of those special persons who take rescue Scotties into their lives will be fortunate enough to experience the love and happiness that our Angus brought to us.

*This chapter by Linda Hill was first published under the same title in *GSM*, Vol 2 No 3 (May/Jun) 1997.

Linda Hill is a Scottie lover, musician, and stock broker in Midland, TX. Today she and husband, Bill, have opened their hearts to two new Scotties.

CHAPTER TWENTY-FIVE

Requiem For A Dog Named Sam

Ani Adhikari

All around him puppies yipped, yapped, jumped, whined, and generally made exhibitions of themselves. The cockapoo bounced up and down like a powderpuff on a trampoline, one yelp per bounce. The miniature pinscher kept up a fierce growling lest passersby dismiss it as a large insect. The golden retriever was doing all she could to co-ordinate the activities of four legs and a tail entirely too big for the rest of her frame. From time to time she gave up the unequal struggle and flopped down mewling in a tangle of limbs.

Through all this he sat perfectly still, oblivious of the din.

His posture would not have impressed a show judge. Back curved, plump bottom planted firmly on the bottom of his cage he sat with one hind leg splayed out, fuzzy ears erect over the massive black head held slightly cocked.

And those eyes. Grave, deep, and watchful, they were filled with the knowledge of the injustice and indignity of his imprisonment. Were they filled also, I wonder now, with a premonition of their fate? At the time I noticed only that his were not doleful, pleading, puppy eyes. They seemed to carry a message but they did not beg. And though the message eluded me I was riveted. Unforgettable, dark as Guinness, Sammy's extraordinary eyes looked back at me and assessed my worth.

"Try your tricks with me," he was saying, "And I'll show you that two can play. Give me credit for some intelligence. Tell me very clearly that you are displeased." I did. "And I will respect that." He did. Photo by A. Adhikari.

All the books I read later said I had picked the wrong dog. The cockapoo, eager to go home with the first person who looked in its direction, had it all over Sam when it came to the social graces. Wrong again to go to a pet store — "Such sources are best avoided," said the most polite of the books. And wrong above all to act on impulse. My friend Joe, euphorically showing off his new Cairn pup, had gushed also about, "the cutest little Scottie in the next cage," so I had to go and see. Wrong three times over, I admit, and plead ignorance and inexperience. Luckily for Sammy and me the gods were forgiving, and the three wrongs combined to make a marvelous right.

He was three months old when I brought him home and ten years and five days old yesterday, when he died. Today the remembering begins.

I would browse the Pets section of every bookstore, riffling through each dog book till I came to the section on Scottish Terriers. "A one-person dog," they said. "Dour but loyal." One of the books rated each breed on various characteristics. "Barking — HIGH," it said of the Scottie. Sammy did love the sound of his own voice. "Obedience — LOW." He would have taken exception to that. Not disobedient, he would have insisted. Just not always unquestioningly obedient.

This was becoming increasingly clear.

"Sammy, sit," I would say.

"No thanks," the dog would reply, face and body language more than compensating for his lack of English.

"Sit, Sam."

"I'm quite happy as I am. Besides, sitting doesn't show off my physique as much as I like. Here, I'll shuffle over and show you my left side. See? Short, dark, and handsome."

"Sammy, SIT!"

"No soul. That's your problem - no soul at all. All right, I'll lower my bottom an inch or so. Satisfied?"

"SITTTT!!"

"I should lift my leg over your Barbara Wodehouse video. A disgrace to her tweeds, that woman. All right, all right, I'm sitting. I'm sitting. Lower your voice, please. My ears are more sensitive than yours."

It took me a few weeks to realize that he usually obeyed in the end, and always co-operated on important matters. He was quick to be housetrained and made no fuss when I left for work. Riding in the car was no problem. Nor was going to bed in his own puppy-carrier away from my bedroom (the books, now lining my shelves, were beginning to have an effect). But practice sessions, recommended by the books and required by his training school, he deemed unnecessary.

"Come, Sam."

"Who, me? What for? It's nice out here. Why don't you come instead, and join me?"

"Sammy, come."

"And why, pray, should I come? I see no effort made in the catering department."

"Sammy!"

"There you go again. You know, your breed is very nice by and large, but stubbornness seems to be one of its traits."

"SAMMY!"

"I'm coming, I'm coming. I heard you the first time. Who do you think I am? Carl Lewis?"

He made sure, of course, that he behaved like an angel at his school. Of the dogs there he was the youngest and by far the cutest, and praise was showered upon him by adoring humans. This he accepted casually as his due, with a few nonchalant waggles of the bottom that said, "Easy peasy. Bring on the badgers."

On most days our lives had a quiet routine — a walk and breakfast, I went to work, he stayed home, I came home, fun and games followed by dinner and another walk, and to bed. Occasionally greater excitement would arrive in the shape of the pizza delivery man, one of the few visitors whom Sammy truly welcomed. But if boredom did set in my dog would provide his own entertainment, all training forgotten.

"If the dog chews the rug," said his trainer (Sammy did), "Put some mustard on it. He won't do it again." They hadn't reckoned with Sammy's gourmand palate. "At last! Condiments!" was his delighted response. "If the dog gets into the garbage," (Sammy did), "Blow up a balloon, attach some bacon grease to it, and put it in the garbage can. The dog will go for the bacon, the balloon will pop, and the terrified dog will never go near the garbage again." It sounded good, so I tried it. The dog went for the bacon. The balloon popped. The dog was thrilled ("At last! Percussion!") and went around to all the other waste baskets looking for more balloons.

"Try your tricks with me," he was saying, "And I'll show you that two can play. Give me credit for some intelligence. Tell me very clearly that you are displeased." I did. "And I will respect that." He did.

He had a point. I did not, after all, communicate with anyone else through the use of mustard or greasy balloons.

The history books I read at school told a story about the young Emperor Alexander who, leading his victorious armies eastward, defeated King Porus in the north of India. Porus, taken prisoner, was asked how he thought Alexander should treat him. "As one king treats another," he answered simply. Moved and impressed, Alexander set him free. Sammy would have approved. He was always a king among kings.

A gruff one-person dog, just as the books said, Sam could nonetheless work up a yapping, panting frenzy in the presence of other dogs. To avoid the "only dog" syndrome deplored by Barbara Wodehouse, and in a greedy effort to replicate Sam, we acquired our second Scottie when Sammy was three years old.

No pet stores this time. The breeder had one black and one wheaten pup, and of course I wanted the black one. But my husband insisted on the wheaten. His clinching argument was, "Or else you'll never know which one to scold."

So Billy arrived, a blond charmer with needle teeth and a winsome sidelong glance. Anxious to please others where Sammy pleased himself, uncertain where Sammy was cocksure, and physical where Sammy was cerebral, he

Sam explores his domain at the Adhikari home, Berkeley, CA. A 1991 wildfire burned the Akhikari home destroying most of the family's belongings-- including early photos of Sam. Pictures for this article supplied by family friends.

was in looks and in character the negative of a snapshot of his hero. Sammy never did concede that the new arrival had any merit.

Not even when Billy began to serve as Sammy's eyes.

It sneaked up on us. At first we put it down to recalcitrance, a more than usual reluctance to pick up the pace during walks. "Come ON, Sam," we would say, ignoring his grumbles. But then he failed to spot a Milk Bone in my hand, and the lengthening shadows of his world reached mine.

"Diagnosis — blindness," said the Animal Eye Specialist unequivocally. He was thorough and businesslike. Blindness was part of a normal day's work.

It remained only to find the cause. Sudden complete loss of sight, like this, could be the result of a tumor in the brain pressing on the occipital nerve. For the few days until the tests were completed I held Sam and scratched his chest and played tug-of-war, overdoing all the ordinary loving things to try and keep from him my throat-tightening anxiety. He was five and a half. His worst health problem to date had been a flea allergy. Dying was not part of our immediate plans.

It was not a tumor. His retinae, both intact, had simply decided not to work any more. A rare condition, cause unknown. It was painless. And irreversible.

Relief that I was not about to lose him swept quickly into despair, then into astonishment and courage as I watched him cope. A couple of sharp knocks taught him not to run. The textures of the floor (carpet in the living room, lino in the kitchen) taught him to find his food. Stairs were harder. We blocked off those inside the house, but he had to negotiate the stairs to the street. Fortunately the treads were low and wide, and he took them slowly one at a time, gingerly pushing his snout over the edge of one to gauge the depth of the next. Each time we praised, coaxed, reassured, congratulated. He learned that, "Step down, Sam," signalled the curb, and that, "Careful!" meant "Stop, then proceed with caution." Who says you can't teach an old dog new tricks?

Did he scream? Did he rage, rage against the dying of the light? Did his deep black chest tremble with bewilderment and pain?

When was the last time he saw my face?

For a while I hoped he would think that we had all gone blind, that some celestial master switch had failed and turned the lights out for everyone. But he knew. And still he carried on, Chief Supervisor of all activities. Expert Commentator on the passing world, First Recipient of all delectables, and Grand Connoisseur of places to sleep. Top Dog.

Poor Billy was mystified. Why was all this attention and praise suddenly being lavished on Sam? More to the point, why was he, Billy, not worthy of the same applause when he performed the very same feats in one-tenth the time? Was slowness the order of the day? Very well, he'd show us. He too could take the stairs one at a time. See, there he was, pausing on each step, head cocked for approval. He could do everything VERY SLOWLY too!

It had not been so long, after all, since they had jointly vanquished their arch enemy, Farley the Dalmatian. Short on brain but large in size and wilfullness, Farley was in complete control of his well-meaning but helpless owner. Despite her best efforts to secure his living quarters he got out regularly. On one of these AWOL excursions he ran into my two dogs who were being taken for their thoroughly legal leash-bound walk. Chaos ensued. Farley grabbed Sam by the scruff of the neck. "No, Farley, NO!" I screamed ineffectually. "No" was not part of Farley's lexicon. But Billy, ever practical, had the solution. He nipped Farley's rear end. Outraged, Farley spun around, thus dropping Sam and leaving him perfectly positioned to nip the other cheek, which he did with vengeful delight. Snarling, Farley turned again, but by this time the two terriers had moved under him and were nibbling away at his soft parts. Farley withdrew. Scotties 1, Dalmatian 0.

Later when Farley took his spotted self for a wander around our steep, scrubby backyard, he would look up and see his conquerors, one black and one white dot bouncing about noisily on the deck high above. The black dot bounced less and made less noise than before. But it was there, and still exuded menace. Farley kept his distance.

Sammy would never admit it, but Billy had become invaluable. It was his excited scampering that signalled someone walking towards the kibble pail. Billy's thundering paws proclaimed an imminent walk, and his preliminary, "Wuf," meant that movement was discernible on the hill below. Never an intellectual giant, Billy would make his announcement and then dance around Sam for advice on the appropriate course of action. "It's the dumb leading the blind," I would say.

Life resumed normalcy. As always, Sammy enjoyed pottering about peacefully at home and in the garden. He received all guests graciously (to Billy, visitors were an unavoidable nuisance, like baths), but later saw them off with a relieved grunt. Fiercely protective of his personal space, Sam had been known to leave the odd toothmark on visiting kids. Adults were more tolerable. But he could react to some with the frigid politeness reserved by the Queen of England for overfriendly heads of emerging nations. If a dull new person decided to pet him, Sammy would first ignore the overture. If the poor fool persisted, Sammy would get up, walk just out of reach and flop down with his back turned implacably towards the offender. Further advances (rarely attempted) he repelled once and for all by embarking upon a delicate but thorough examination of his own genitalia.

Blindness made him more appreciative of petting, and he unnerved several guests by burrowing between the sofa and the backs of their legs, squirming and groaning with pleasure. Baths and hairbrushing became sensual occasions. He would lie back and wallow in our attentions like a Roman emperor being plied with grapes by nubile young beauties.

Would he have classified himself as a dog? Surely not. He was, he believed, neither dog nor human but a superior creature with the rights and privileges of both. I dare to think that in his view I too was part of this superbreed.

It is said that dogs and their owners often resemble each other, and Sammy and I had much in common. "Short, smart, and stubborn," would have described each of us equally. "Scruffy," too, perhaps — we were not highly coiffed. Sam was shorn twice a year at home, and then he looked like

Marjorie Flack's Angus. The rest of the time he looked like Fala. Very handsome he was either way, as he would have been the first to point out.

We were quite a picture, Sam and I, plodding along on our walks. A large construction worker, watching us in amazement from his large truck in which he was restraining his large dog, concluded, "Well I guess short people must like short dogs."

There was never any thought of creating more Sams, even in the days when he was brimming with good health. His only encounter with a female dog in season had ended ignominiously. He knew that he was supposed to be interested but was puzzled by exactly what to do, so he spent some time examining the front end of his ladyfriend before he was removed amid much derisive laughter. It was just as well, or else the world may have been inflicted with a cross between Sammy and a wire-haired Dachshund.

Sam's blindness doesn't affect his olfactory senses as he checks for goodies at the Adhikari home. Photo by A. Adhikari.

Day by day Sammy continued to astonish. We moved house, with me worried that he would be mystified and frightened. I should have known better. Within days Sammy was master of his new domain, indignantly snuffling at doors that had been shut to simplify his new maze. He knew that he had to avoid running indoors, but once his feet touched the grass outside he was off. Bounce, bounce, bounce, with yaps of delight, clearly thinking he was running miles. We could see of course that he was bouncing almost in place, but who is to say that our reality was more real than his?

A mouse made the mistake of getting too close to Sammy's personal flower pots. Blindness notwithstanding Sammy soon got rid of it while Billy scurried around trying to look useful. When unpicked cherry tomatoes dropped off the overabundant vine Sam was ready. He would stand with his front paws on the planter and delicately extract a single jewel-like fruit from the mulch. Then he would drop to the ground, savor the morsel, and repeat the process. If we lived in Tuscany I could have used him to look for truffles.

All was joy, until the day I called him and he scampered eagerly in the direction exactly opposite to where I was. I was bewildered, and Sam resentful that I was playing tricks on him. Why was I not where my voice was? It soon became clear that while his hearing was still sharp, he could not place the direction of a sound. A cruel blow to a blind dog, and, as always with Sammy, a mystery to the vets. One by one they looked at him and uttered the dreaded, "Hmm, very interesting!" And so once again Sammy and I had to find ways to cope. He could follow handclaps better than voices so I learned to keep my mouth shut. As before, his intelligence helped to overcome the disability. He knew that his ears could mislead, so upon hearing his name he would take a single step and wait for the verdict of, "No, other way," or, "Good!" from me. The next step he would adjust accordingly.

Mercifully this condition was not continuous, and there were days when he knew exactly where all the sounds were. Then just as suddenly he'd be "turned around" again. All hail the unjustly named Dr. Richard Hack for solving the problem with a thyroid pill. We needed all the help we could get. The constant battles with his own senses were beginning to weaken Sam.

Other ills of age were creeping up. His mouth needed attention, he had a tumor, and surgery was required more than once to prevent discomfort. After Sam recovered from one of his operations I invited him to come along on his

usual walk. For the first time in his life he refused. He stood stock still in the path, ears and tail down, fearing that this walk, like another recent one, would lead to the car and the vet and pain and strange hands and unknown darkness like the pits of hell. I cajoled, offered reassurance, and begged him to come. Miserable, my brave little dog shook with terror, all dignity abandoned.

And then, all hope abandoned too, he came. Trembling, legs barely able to move, he came, because I asked him to.

"Obedience — LOW," my foot. His joy when he realized that this was really just an ordinary walk will stay with me for the rest of my days.

Three days ago we took our last walk, Sam and I. Slowly we went up the path, Sam's movements stiff but determined. There to comfort us were all the familiar smells, the well-known textures underfoot, the usual neighborhood sounds. We stayed close to home and came back when he was tired. We were at peace, and for a little while we let ourselves forget that the tumor was winning.

Rest, my Sam. Forgive the dumb human inhibitions that kept me from joining Billy last night when he went out and howled his lament to the skies. I know now what you were telling me with your eyes that first day in the pet store. "I am small," you were saying, "And I am caged and vulnerable. But I am someone, and I am worthy of your respect."

I hope I was worthy of yours.

*This chapter by Ani Adhikari was first published under the same title in *GSM*, Vol 4 No 1 (Jan/Feb) 1999.

Ani Adhikari teaches statistics at the University of California, Berkeley. She grew up in India, and her passion for Scotties goes back to her childhood when her mother brought her a stuffed black Scottie all the way from Edinburgh. Ani lives in Berkeley with her husband Jim, son Ian, and wheaten Scottie Billy, who has taken on the role of Chief Dog with great aplomb.

Afterword

"The fidelity of a dog is a precious gift demanding no less binding moral responsibilities than the friendship of a human being. The bond with a true dog is as lasting as the ties of this earth can ever be."

Konrad Lorenz

A Parable For Our Times

Today I bring truths old and new, truths from the dark ages of Scottie beginnings never recorded in your history books. Part legend, part myth, part fancy, this tale is only whispered at gatherings of the Old Ones, for here is the collective memory of the Great Crisis at the dawn of Scottie history, and of our darkest hour.

I am Hoary MacTerrier, Venerable Keeper of the Tale, of the Clan MacTerrier. I am Gatekeeper of Yesteryear and Guardian of Scottie wisdom past and present, and I break the code of Scottie Silence on these Mysteries not to castigate my Clan but to educate all Two-Leggeds whose ways in matters of loyalty bear resemblance to our own dark beginnings. Perhaps by my revelation you can better understand why things are as they are today between Scotties and their people. For the stalwart, loyal Scottie you know well— I say it with anguish— was not always so. And in the secret of our Great Crisis and its lesson of loyalty is the tragedy of Scottie wisdom hard-won! So if you've wondered why Scotties look

Drawing by Larry Anderson

the way we do, why we love the way we do, my Tale of Beginnings will answer. For those with ears to hear my tale reveals why my Clan is so troubled today by values and choices we see among our Persons. Because we know the Mysteries, we warn of consequences.

My theme is *loyalty*— than which is no greater term in our Scottie language. To grasp this term, to know its awful burden in our dark and secret past, is to grasp the Scottie soul; to trivialize it is to miss the lesson of life.

The Mystery of Loyalty takes us back beyond the days of the Old Ones, beyond history itself, to the Great Whelping and to a place the Ancients called, Halcyon. It was there the Great Spirit, out of her great-souled love of companionship, created all things to share her world in joy. But for herself she created a special companion. The Great Spirit created a Scottie.

Our sacred legend tells of their special union— the Great Spirit and her Scottie, the two of them together in all things. They were one in naming all the animals and creatures of the earth. And the Great Spirit gave her Scottie dominion over all of Halcyon and over all the creatures in the Land. And to the Scottie she said, "And you shall be called *'Terri-Ur,'* (which loosely translated means 'first-in-loyalty') for you are spirit of my Spirit, and you shall be a testament of faithfulness for all creation."

And Terri-Ur was fruitful and multiplied and filled Halcyon with the joy of many litters. And the Great Spirit created Persons to keep Terri-Ur company, saying, "In my absence these shall be to you as you are to Me: parable close and small of true communion."

And all was well in Halcyon: no wants, no strife. Those were the days of joy and union!

In time the Great Spirit went away to create other worlds. She left her Scotties in charge of Halcyon, confident of Terri-Ur's loyalty and devotion.

Legend says all went well for a time.

But one day there came a stranger. He drifted into Halcyon, part plant and part animal and part person. His name was *Canid*, which in the ancient tongue of Halcyon was a term of respect.

At first the Stranger seemed kind, but soon he began planting evil notions in the hearts and minds of the Scotties of Halcyon. He seduced us with new ideas from worlds far away, with wonderments he called 'freedom,' 'rights,' and 'independence.' Gradually his mood shifted from extolling the virtues of greener grass elsewhere to vilifying self-sacrifice and the constraints of Halcyon.

In the beginning scarcely any Scotties paid attention to the Stranger. But over time —I say it to our immortal shame— we listened! All came under the spell of Canid, even Terri-Ur himself.

Things changed in Halcyon. The long and elegant legs given to us in the Beginning by the Great Spirit— long and graceful legs to match Her stride in faithful unison— now became tools for promiscuity, wandering in search of personal gratification. Young Scotties began to despise Halcyon as repressive and they longed only for some distant country. We became fickle and our consciences were turned to stone.

The Great Crisis came when our hearts were so poisoned by the lies of the Stranger that we no longer cared even for our Persons whom the Great Spirit gave us as companions. Legend tells of a crisis of neglect so evil there arose in Halcyon a futile program called 'Person Rescue' where wicked Scotties dumped unwanted Persons, and where dark and unspeakable things were done to helpless, unloved human companions!

It was a crisis of neglect and violence beyond telling. The loyalty which is our very name was renounced in unbridled self-interest.

When the Great Spirit returned to Halcyon She was devestated by the betrayal of her beloved Scotties. When she saw the selfishness and disloyalty in the land she uttered a heart-stopping wail as hot tears rolled from her face to scorch the earth like molton lava. So mournful was that wail, so awesome its cry of grief and heartbreak, it stopped every Scottie in the land dead in their tracks. To this day the wail of a siren haunts us with atavistic memories of our darkest hour.

The Great Spirit gathered before her all creation and judged Halcyon for its wickedness.

She decreed that henceforth Halcyon itself should become only a dim dream.

To the Stranger she said, "For your evil lies and influence you shall be cursed to roam the earth in search of a friend. Your very name shall be a hiss and a by-word among Persons; they shall be your Master, and your peril shall be at their hands."

And to all the animals she said, "You have defiled our covenant and broken my heart. You are no longer worthy sovereigns. From this day forward you, too, shall know forever the bitter taste of neglect. Persons shall be your rulers and the lash your heritage."

Then the Great Spirit turned to Terri-Ur. "Because you, my own companion, listened to Canid's lies, your folly is greater than the rest. From this day forward your burden shall be a heart the size of a mountain that will never again be your own but shall always belong to another. From henceforth your graceful, elegant legs by which you have led Halcyon into ruin shall be stumps and parodies to teach you the folly of a wandering heart. You shall remember sacred beginnings and the bitter memory will teach you the ruin of pride."

She paused and uttered again the wail of a broken heart. Finally, in words scarcely audible, she whispered, "But I have loved you with a great love, and for the sake of the memory of our Beginnings and the goodness I know is in your heart, your destiny shall be secure. The Persons who shall rule over you will not know of Halcyon so they will see you as you were in the Beginning and as you shall become. You shall be what I made you to be: paragon of loyalty. Wherever Persons speak of faithfulness they shall speak your name. But your destiny shall be at great cost. Henceforth sovereignty will be for you a haunting memory for from this day on your heart shall never again be your own; you will never be whole except in the company of your special Person to whom you will belong."

And so the world changed. Even the memory of those dreadful events has mercifully faded, and Persons now tell very different versions of the Great Whelping. But my Tale is true as it was vouchsafed to me by the Elders as handed down from the Old Ones.

Now the dark and terrible Tale is told of our lesson in loyalty. These are the Mysteries of our past; the prologue of our future. To know our sacred tale is to understand our secret burden; it is to know how and why relations are as they are today between Scotties and their People. More importantly, it is to know why we love with a fierce and exclusive love. Loyalty for us is more than a notion. Loyalty is our Destiny.

So the next time you see a Scottie with a melancholy face lost in silent contemplation, it is likely you are observing unconscious signs of the Mysteries at work in the depths of that Scottie's soul. Private reveries are all we now have of our lost Halcyon. When you ponder your Scottie's large head, or marvel at her truncated legs; or the next time he wails at a siren, or you puzzle over your dog's legs twitching as she dreams of wanderings in our collective past, recall my sober words and the Tale of Halcyon.

If you look closely at your Scottie and if you have ears to hear the words Life would put to you, you can discover the wisdom we embody and the truth we bring to you at great cost. Perhaps before it is too late your human world can learn from our past the ruin of self-centeredness. Perhaps, while there is still time, you can learn that companions are sacred; that loyalty is job #1.

Original art by Elena Lettelier commissioned by Tartan Scottie. ©1997 Tartan Scottie.

* This chapter is a revised version of *'All I Need To Know About Life I Learned From My Scottie (Scottie Wisdom No. 2): Loyalty Is Job #1'* by Joseph Harvill, which first appeared in **Great Scots Magazine,** Vol 1 No 4 (Jul/Aug, 1996).

Appendix
Select Breed Bibliography

Best of the Old Scottie Books

D.J. Thomson Gray, ***The Dogs of Scotland: Their Varieties, History, Characteristics, and Exhibition Points***. Edinburgh: James P. Mathew, 1891, 220 pp. This book is uniquely important because it preserves the only known excerpts of Captain W.W. Mackie's travel diary written in the 1870s when Mackie scoured the Western Highlands of Scotland for prime breeding stock of the then little known "Scotch Terrier."

C.J. Davies, ***The Scottish Terrier***. London: Everett & Co., n.d. (c. 1906), 121 pp. Davies' book has many wonderful photos of turn-of-the-century Scotties, and important early pedigree charts. His history sections, 'remote' and 'modern,' are important.

W.L. McCandlish, ***The Scottish Terrier***. Manchester, England: Our Dogs Pub. Co., n.d. (c. 1910), 66 pp. plus 30 illustrations. McCandlish offers insights into the origins of the name "Aberdeen Terrier" as well as other important perspectives on the early history of our breed.

Dorothy Gabriel, ***The Scottish Terrier: Its Breeding and Management***. London: Dog World, Ltd., n.d. (c. 1930), 60 pp. plus 10 plates. Gabriel is one of the best of the early writers at capturing in words the character and spirit of the Scottie. She makes you think, and it's always good thoughts!

Dr. William A. Bruette, ***The Scottish Terrier***. New York: G. Howard Watt, 1934, 224 pp. Bruette's book is encyclopedic. His chapter on "Terrier Facts & Fancies" is a look into Scottie politics of the 1930s through Bruette's jaundiced appraisal of the push at that time to 'fox terrier-ize' the Scottie's head shape. Insightful chapters on history are worth the price of the book.

Fayette C. Ewing, ***The Book of the Scottish Terrier: With Chapters Applicable to the Hygenic Care, Rearing, and Treatment of all Dogs***. New York: Orange Judd, Inc., 1932, 251 pp. I consider Ewing's book the best— perhaps the best Scottie book ever written. He had the discipline and skills of a true scholar, the heart of a poet, and the experience of a life-long love affair with Scotties. He was concerned over color fads and faddish breeding and took pains to document and preserve early records and histories of our breed. Listening to him through his pages the thoughtful reader hears one who has earned the right to be heard. Ewing's book went through many editions. It can be found in better second-hand bookshops and is well worth whatever you pay for it.

Best of the Modern Scottie Books (Alphabetical Order)

Cindy Cooke, *The New Scottish Terrier*. NY: Howell Book House, 1996. Helpful diaglott comparison of breed standards past and present.

Muriel P. Lee, *The Official Book of the Scottish Terrier*. Neptune City, NJ: T.F.H. Publications, 1994. Sanctioned by the Scottish Terrier Club of America this is a comprehensive book with lavish color photos. Important health and diseases section.

John T. Marvin, *The New Complete Scottish Terrier*. NY: Howell Book House, 1982. 2nd edition. Cindy Cooke's book (above) replaces Marvin in the Howell series, but in history and broad usefulness Marvin is superior.

Betty Penn-Bull, *The Kennelgarth Scottish Terrier Book*, reprinted in a 2nd edition (1995), 340 pp., by The Scottish Emergency Care Scheme (British Scottie Rescue), Berkshire, England. This book, an expanded version of the 1983 edition, is encyclopedic, distilling the author's many decades of intimate Scottie research, highly acclaimed breeding, and pioneering experience with our breed. There is more practical counsel on Scottie breeding, health and welfare in this book than can be found anywhere else. Betty Penn-Bull's champion Kennelgarth Scotties, her definitive textbook on the breed, and her amazing longevity in British Scottie circles, make her a living legend among Scottie lovers. The Penn-Bull book sells for $75.00, proceeds fund the British Scottie Rescue, and can be ordered from England. Contact Nellie Holland, Noonsun Kennels, Woodside Farm, Everest Road, Hyde, Cheshire SK14 4DX, England, U.K.

T.H. Snethen, *Scottish Terriers*. Neptune City, NJ: T.F.H. Publications, 1995. Useful beginners book which incorporates some of the earlier, excellent little book by Mr. and Mrs. T.H. Snethen (1956), long out of print.

Where To Look

Three good resources for old Scottie books are: Bern Marcowitz at **Dog Lovers Bookshop** (New York City) 212/369-7554, or you may e-mail info@dogbooks.com; Viola Neill at **4-M Enterprises** (Union City, CA) 800-487-9867; Kathy Darling at **Dog Ink** (Larchmont, NY) 914/ 834-9029, or e-mail dogink@aol.com.

Remember: the joy of great books is not acquisitiveness; the prize is participating in the on-going conversation of great ideas. Collecting important books and never reading them is obscene and doubly obscene when non-readers hoard old, scarce books. If you find them, read them, and share with others what you learn about the magic of Scottish Terriers.

Index

A

A Scottie much-loved never dies
   poem 119
Adamec, Christine
   canine death & grieving 156
Adhikari, Ani 165
Affirming words
   role of in companionship 35
American Kennel Club 31
Angus MacTavish 160
Argos 150
Argyle Hopscotch Buckingham 100
Art
   extravagance of 40
   Scotties as fine 39
ArtPaw 44

B

Baby
   Scotties and 77
Baer, Nancy & Steve Duno 71
Balcom, Deborah 77
Bark
   know when to 91
Barton, Bob 151
Betweenness
   perspective of 33
Bird Dog
   a Scottie bird dog 121
Biting
   control of 70
   Scotties and 70
Blackstone, Doreen 24
Bladder Cancer
   frequency in Scotties 41
   strategies for fighting 98
   test 99
Blindness
   story of Scottie 169
Body language
   importance of reading 37
Bonding
   relation of to discipline 30
Bookshop, Dog Lovers vii, 183
Bootcamp
   puppy 61
Breeders
   locating information about 60
Brody, Jane 25
Bruette, Dr. William A. 17, 182
Buber, Martin 43

C

Caledonia, Land of 12
Cancer
   living with Scottie 94
Canine groups
   Stanley Coren's new categories 48
Caras, Roger 39
Carlson, Jeanne & Ranny Green 31
Case Study
   Balcom Family
      model Scottie integration 77
Check-list
   breeder rating 57, 58
Chemotherapy
   cancer treatment and 95
Clean up
   dog owner's responsibility to 86
Commitment
   role of in companionship 35
Communication
   role of in companionship 35
Company "G" 146
Conditioning
   importance of reinforcement in 69
Contracts
   breeder's use of 63

Control
    essential to dog-walking 84
Cooke, Cindy 18
Coren, Dr. Stanley
    research of
        theory on breed matching 47
Correlation
    of Scotties and homeland 12f.

D

Darling, Kathy 183
Davies, C.J. 182
Dawson, Marcia
    bladder cancer test 99
'Demon' Puppy
    on loving the 72
Die-hard
    Scotties as 15, 19, 40
Distress
    damsel in 114
Dog
    shortcourse in walking the 83
Dog Power
    modern canine status 152
Dog-lish
    canine language of 31
Dominance
    personality dimension of 52
Don Quixote 22, 119
Dumbbell
    bird hunting tool 122

E

Economic models
    peril of for viewing life 40
Empathy
    importance of in family models 80
Esquire
    Scottie as gentleman's 23
Ethos
    of Scotties and homeland 12
Ewing, Fayette C. 17, 182
Example
    need for owners to set a good 86
Extravagance
    Scotties as symbols of 40
Extroversion
    personality dimension of 51

F

Fala
    F.D.R.'s Scottie 22
Family
    shrinking of modern 153
Finn, Rex Weldon 17
Formal Training
    Scotties' need for 71
Fragile
    Scottie as 40

G

Gabriel, Dorothy 23
Gannon, Robert 59
Garber, Marjorie 156
Gear, Mabel
    drawing by 40
Gene pool
    fragility of Scottie's 41
General Wade 14
Gilman, Sally 107, 110, 111, 112
Giving Back
    rescue as opportunity for 108
God
    Scotties and 43f.
God's Administrative Assistant 136
Good dogs
    definition of 27
Good Dogs Are Made 25
Good Life
    celebrating the 113
    celebrating the Scottie 149
Good Owners
    characteristics of 29
Goodness
    "fragility of" 40
Gray, D.J. Thomson 17, 182
Gus 23, 37

H

Habhab, Anver 140
Hadrian's Wall 15
Hart, B.L. and L.A. 25
Harvill, Joseph 12, 18, 25, 32,
    38, 47, 72, 77, 88, 101, 115,
    121, 132, 137, 141, 151, 177

Health Care
  preventive 67
Hearne, Vicki 37
Highland "clearances" 11, 15
Hill, Linda 160
Hoary MacTerrier 176
Home
  Scotties as symbol of 42
Homeless boy
  story of 112
Homemade Good 30
Homer 150
Humanizing
  Scotties and our 29
Hume, David. 13, 16
Hurt
  why so much? 150
Hyland, 'Tunia' 131

I

Immediate Gratification
  reward of 105
Imperfection
  in praise of
    poem to Nati 120
Independent
  Scottie trait of 21
Inner Space
  Scotties as symbols of 41
Inventory
  Scottie seeker's personal 61

J

Jet
  paraplegic Scottie 127
"June Bug"
  therapy Scottie 131

K

King George I 14
Knowledge
  key to safe dog-walking 85
Knox, John 13

L

Lee, Muriel P. 183
Little Things
  power of 102
Loss
  coping with Scottie 150
Love Letter 157
Loving Well
  the art of 100
Loyalty
  legend of 176

M

M.Y.S.T.I.Q.U.E
  the Scottie 18
Mackie, J.D. 17
Maller, Dick & Jeffrey Feinman 71
Marchi, Lt. Col. B.G. 146
Marvin, John T. 183
Maynard, Kate 43
McAfee, Ginger 61
McCandlish, W.L. 182
McKnight
  a distressed damsel and 114
Memories
  role of in companionship 34
Model
  Balcom Family
    Jack and newborn, Rebecca 78
Moral
  lessons from puppy raising 73
Mystery
  Scotties and 19
Myths
  shattering of modern 154

N

Nash, Nicholas 127
Nati 23, 36, 37, 114
  eleven rules for living 88
Neill, Viola 183
Netzler, Lee 83, 121, 157
  photo of 85, 86, 87, 126
Nieburg, Herbert A. & Arlene Fischer
  pet loss 156

Nurturing
  the Scottie good life 46
Nussbaum, Martha 40

O

Obedience
  puppies and 68
Odysseus 150f.
"Old vets never die"
  poem to shorty 148
Olson, John T. 71
Olson, Terry 111
On Loving Angus
  a journey of the heart 160
Other-ness
  discovery of 21
Owen, Carole Fry 56

P

Pace
  importance of in family integration 82
Pain
  a look inside Scottie loss 150
Parable
  for our times 176
Parallels of Courage 15
Parallels of Independence 16
Parallels of Loyalty & Affection 14
Parallels of Size 13
Paraplegic Scottie
  essentials list for a 130
Perceptions
  negative: re: Scotties 26
Personality test
  for human/canine matching 49f.
Piroxicam
  treatment for bladder cancer 98
Plato 20
Positivity
  place of in Scottie discipline 81
Psyche
  canine as symbol in human psyche 45
Puppy
  bringing home a new 64
  finding the right Scottie 56
  first night care of 64

Purpose
  rescue as source of 109

Q

Quixote, Don 22
Quixotic
  Scottie trait of 22

R

Rating Scale
  personality test 50
Rating Score Card
  for personality test 51
Reciprocity
  role of in Scottie/baby introductions 80
Reid, Thomas 13
Reputable breeders
  practices of 60, 63
Research
  importance of in fighting cancer 98
Respect
  role of in introducing new babies 80
Rewards
  the pay-offs of Scottie love 104
Risks
  while dog-walking 84
Rules
  for responsible dog-walking 84
Rusty
  bird dog with a brogue 121

S

Sagacity
  Scottie trait of 20
Sales agreement
  reputable breeders' use of 58
Sam
  requiem for a dog named 165
Savior Roles
  rescue as opportunity for 106
Scotland 12
  Dog of 12
Scotland's history 12f.
Scottie
  instant
    woes of 59

Scottie angels 33, 119
Scottie Cramp 58, 63
Scottie Crazies 32, 153
Scottie pet
   cost of 60
Scottie Quotient
   self-test 47
Scottie Rescue 29
   rewards of 106
Scottie World
   cartoon: "Sit, stay, heel" 28
   cartoon: 'Squirrely' 30
ScottiePhile
   on-line Scottie health resource 99
Scottily
   rules for growing old 88
Scottish Terrier
   As definitive export 12
      mirroring owner 12
Scottish Terrier Club of America 56
Seamus
   bladder cancer Scottie 94
Security Blanket
   Scotties as 154
Sellers, Ronnie 37
Senior
   85 year-old
      on living life over again 34
Shadows
   redeeming the 149
Shalloe, Marki 94
Shawnee Indian
   story of creation 38
Sheena 163
Shepard, Paul 45
Shorty
   WWII mascot named 140
Siegal, Mordecai 71
Sir Alexander Gray
   Poem by 17
Smith, Adam 13
Snethen, T.H. 183
Socialization
   young Scotties' need for 67
Spay or neuter 57, 64
STCA
   Scottish Terrier Club of America 41, 60

STCA Rescue
   contact information for 60
Stewart, John 33
Stories
   Scotties as evokative of 42
Storyteller
   man as 42
Sunshine
   recounting the days of 113
Synergy
   between Scotties and owners 33

T

Tags
   first rule of dog-walking 84
Terri-Ur 177
Terrier
   Scotties as quintessential 21
Test Match-Up
   graphic for 53
The Land 12
The Odyssey 151
The Republic
   Plato's book of 20
The Road
   only a bump in the 127
Theology
   Scotties as invitations to practice 43
Therapy
   'June Bug' 131
Thinkers
   Scotties as 20
Thurston, Mary 152, 156
Ties That Bind 32
Today
   importance of in loving well 101
Toffler, Alvin 155, 156
Toilet Training
   new puppies and 65
Trickett, Pam 136
Trust
   personality dimension of 52
Twain, Mark 107, 175

U

Unique
   Scottie as 22

V

Van Dine, S.S. 20, 22
Visit
   on-site 62
Volhard, Jack & Melissa Bartlett 31
vonWillebrand's Disease 58

W

Warmth
   personality dimension of 53
Watt, James 13
Webb, Stephen H. 45
'Wee Willie' 23, 36, 37, 72
   antics of 72
   photo at 16 weeks 73
   photo of today 76
Wendt, Lloyd M. 156

Wesley 132, 133
Wickersham, Doris 60
Wiggins, Jerry S. 49
Wisdom
   for the new millennium 38
Woloy, Eleanora M.
   canine as symbol in psyche 45

Y

Yesterday
   Scotties shaped by 19
Yield
   essential to dog-walking manners 86

Z

Zoe
   Scottie named 136

Also from Tartan Scottie

Great Scots magazine

The ground-breaking magazine that defines the genre of Scottie celebration!

♥Critically acclaimed writing celebrating Scotties as companions covers Scottish Terrier health, socialization, history, travel, literature, humor, Scottie Rescue, and more. Winner of Dog Writers Association of America's 1999 Maxwell Medallion for 'Best Article In A Single Breed Publication.'

♥Bi-monthly magazine bringing 6 issues per year *by* Scottie lovers, *for* Scottie lovers, filled with Scottie-specific wit and wisdom not found anywhere else.

♥Each issue a 'collectible,' subscribers call *GSM* "chicken soup for the soul of everyone who was ever owned by a Scottie!"

Tartan Scottie

| 1-800-766-6091 | 1028 Girard Blvd., NE | 505/ 266-7211 |
| www.tartanscottie.com | Albuquerque, NM 87106-2048 | scottie@tartanscottie.com |

Also from Tartan Scottie

VHS Video

"... You'll laugh, and you'll cry, but most of all you will celebrate with new passion the dogs that own your heart!"

The

Scottie

M.Y.S.T.I.Q.U.E

by
Joseph Harvill, Ph.D.

With award-winning insight the publisher of *Great Scots Magazine* narrates his definitive look into the great-souled character of the Scottish Terrier. Going beyond breed standards, this 30 minute VHS video captures in words, music, and photos the magic between Scotties and their people. Here is a banquet for the senses of the highest order, an unforgettable celebration for the Scottie lover's mind, heart, and will.

$20.00 (USD)
plus shipping

VISA **MasterCard**

Tartan Scottie

1-800-766-6091
www.tartanscottie.com

1028 Girard Blvd., NE
Albuquerque, NM 87106-2048

505/ 266-7211
scottie@tartanscottie.com

New from Tartan Scottie

'Songs of the Aberdeen'

Audio tapes of
Great Scottish Terrier stories
from the pages of
Great Scots Magazine

$18.00 (USD)
boxed set
plus shipping

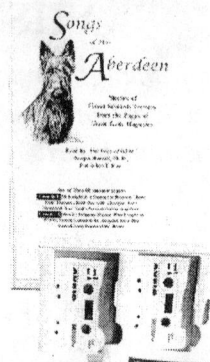

VISA MasterCard

Recordings of favorite stories of Scotties and their people as you always wanted to hear them! Read by Joseph Harvill, publisher/editor of *Great Scots Magazine*, these selected stories dramatize the love at the heart of Scottie magic.

- ♥ Two 60 minute cassettes in a boxed set.

  - ♥ Stories: 'McKnight & A Damsel In Distress,' 'Bird Dog With A Brogue,' 'June Bug Therapy,' 'Love Returned,' 'Zoe: God's Administrative Assistant,' 'Requiem For A Dog Named Sam,' 'Shorty: WWII Mascot,' 'The Art of Loving Well,' plus limmericks & poems to warm your heart.

    - ♥ Perfect for the commuter: turn highway miles into Scottie smiles listening to classic stories of unforgettable Scotties!

      - ♥ Every Scottie ›ver's quintessential 'bed-time stories'— hear tl m again for the first time!

Tartan Scottie

1-800-766-6091
www.tartanscottie.com

1028 Girard Blvd., NE
Albuquerque, NM 87106-2048

505/ 266-7211
scottie@tartanscottie.com